The Zeroth Apple

-Manifest your Abundant YOUniverse

Omkara Cheetrala

First Published in Month 2023

ISBN:

Price: INR

BLUEROSE PUBLISHERS
www.bluerosepublishers.com
info@bluerosepublishers.com
+91 8882 898 898

Cover Design:
Name

Typographic Design:
Name

Editor:
Name

Distributed by: BlueRose, Amazon, Flipkart

DISCLAIMERS

i. This book is for your learning use only. Any trademarked names, books, or literature mentioned in this book are the sole property of their respective companies, authors, publishers, or owners. None of these companies are associated with the Author or Publisher.

ii. All characters mentioned in this book unless mentioned with birth and death years after their names are fictional, any resemblance to real persons, living or dead is pure coincidence.

iii. Neither the publisher nor the author shall be held liable or responsible for any loss or damage allegedly arising from any suggestion or information contained in this book.

iv. The information in this book is true and complete to the best of our knowledge. All recommendations are made without guarantee by the author or Publisher. The author and Publisher declaim any liability in connection with the use of this information.

v. The results are not typical. Individual results may vary. The testimonials, statements, and opinions mentioned or quoted in this book apply to the individuals. Results will vary and may not be those of others.

DEDICATION

I'd like to dedicate this book to all those who would like to create their YOUniverses with ease and make this planet a great place to live.

I would also like to express my gratitude and dedicate a significant portion of this book to my virtual mentors, who never spoke to me directly but, through their speeches and books, have inspired me to become a better writer and a better person.

Dedicated to you, who wonders if I am writing to you. Yes, I am.!

ACKNOWLEDGEMENT

I want to take this opportunity to acknowledge the following individuals and entities who have contributed to the creation of this book:

Firstly, my publisher, who supported me throughout the entire process of marketing and designing this book's cover.

To the people who created challenging situations in my life that inspired me to complete this book, I thank you for the challenges that helped me grow and develop as an individual.

I would also like to acknowledge my friends who never helped me in tough times, as it was their absence that forced me to become the strongest version of what I am today.

To my managers, who always made me feel small, thank you for motivating me to prove you wrong and complete this book.

Last but not least, I would like to acknowledge my Lord, Shiva, my guardian, for his unwavering support and guidance throughout my life's journey.

PREFACE

Welcome to "*The Zeroth Apple: Manifest your Abundant YOUniverse*", a condensed version of my years of research and fieldwork on Human Psychological Well Being and Achieving Success as a 360 Degree Life Transforming Success and Abundance Coach.

Throughout the pages of this book, we will explore how the power of the mind and spirit can be harnessed to achieve success and improve overall health and well-being. Whether you seek greater happiness, financial prosperity, or personal fulfilment, the teachings and principles presented in this book will provide the tools and guidance you need to reach your full potential.

So, if you're ready to take control of your life and start living the life you deserve, join us on this journey and discover the power of mind and spirit. Together, we will explore the secrets of success and well-being and learn how to harness the power within to create the life of our dreams.

This is not any other book; you will read it today. This is the only book you may have to read if this is the last hour of your life.

INTRODUCTION

Have you ever seen someone with a magical touch? As if their dumbest decisions also fall into place only to bring the best of their life moments to reality?

It's not some Aladdin's lamp that only one could possess that they have it with them, it is within you, me, and everyone around us, including us.

Yes, the genie, the ultimatum, the supreme power: The Brain and The Spirit. We all have them but don't know how to use them to our advantage and get whatever we want.

Buckle up for a roller coaster ride throughout the pages of this book. You may learn some new philosophies that could shatter your old beliefs or find some interesting theories you may have never heard or couldn't even see in the future.

This book won't give you the Alladin's lamp; rather, you will become the Genie, who could manifest his/ her own YOUniverse.

TABLE OF CONTENTS

PART ONE:

INTRODUCTION

CHAPTER 1:
ONCE UPON A TIME...

David's Story:

David was born into a family that struggled to make ends meet and made their home on a reservation in the more rural parts of the Southwest. It had always been difficult for him to make ends meet and provide for his family, and he frequently had the impression that he was caught in a cycle of poverty that would never end.

Even though things were hard for David, he never gave up hope and never wavered in his determination to improve things. He was determined to attend the seminar he had heard about from his friend, which promised to teach people how to take their lives from good to great.

David was aware that it would be difficult for him to afford the ticket as well as the travel costs for the seminar because it was being held in a major city. However, he was determined to make a change in his life, so he scrounged together every last penny he had and embarked on the journey.

David was in the audience, listening to the different speakers. One of the speakers' stories moved him in a particular way. This man also came from humble beginnings and struggled to make ends meet. However, he turned his life around by using the power of the law of attraction, the power of the subconscious mind, and self-hypnosis. He called this technique "Apple," which David can't quite recall.

After hearing the speaker's story, David was very moved and immediately felt a strong connection with him. He knew that if this man had been able to overcome problems and be successful, then he might be able to do the same.

During the lunch break, David discovered that he was seated next to a businesswoman named Sarah. Sarah had been through a divorce, and despite her best efforts, she could not find happiness or contentment in her personal life.

She tended to date men who were dishonest and couldn't be trusted, and she was starting to lose hope that she would ever find a partner who would genuinely love and respect her.

David and Sarah discovered, during the course of their conversation over lunch, that they shared a lot of similarities. They were both struggling to create the lives they wanted, and they found inspiration in the story that the speaker shared with them.

Following lunch, David and Sarah decided to go for a walk so that they could both get some fresh air and process everything that they had just heard. They were walking when they ran into the speaker, who recognized them from the earlier seminar.

They discussed how well they connected with the speaker's story. However, due to their current states of mind, they were unable to fully believe, or rather, trust, the teachings they learned in the seminar that day. All their great future was being blocked, and their vision was being fogged by the two most dangerous killers of all hopes: "Self-doubt" and "Skepticism."

Easier done than said to understand:

The speaker, John, was deeply moved by his connection with David and Sarah during his presentation. Due to his long career mentoring people and understanding their psyches, he can clearly see the skepticism on their faces. He wanted to show them the strategies that had been instrumental in his life's transformation and assist them in putting those strategies into practice in their own lives in the here and now, so he invited them to dinner.

John helped David and Sarah understand the concepts of visualization by having them do several different exercises to help them picture their desired future. During these exercises, both Sarah and David were told to imagine having the things they wanted in their lives already and to focus on those things.

By the time they were able to reach a level of understanding and confidence in the space of visualization, John's wife called them for lunch.

After eating, they kept learning about the power of the subconscious mind and how it affects what we think and do. John led them through the process of self-hypnosis so they could change the limiting beliefs and thought patterns that had been ingrained in their subconscious minds.

John noticed that David was picking up the teachings quickly, but somewhere Sarah was left behind after lunch. David had a habit of talking to his family after lunch whenever he was away from family, so while he was excused to call his family, John started a conversation with Sarah to understand what happened.

Sarah opened up and expressed her concern about attracting all betrayed partners, and she felt so jealous of John's wife having John as her husband. David said nothing to her but continued to help them understand the different techniques he employs in his life to make his life lively and colorful.

After practicing their skills over and over again, David and Sarah started to understand how they could use these strategies to change their lives. They were filled with optimism and excitement about the changes they were already beginning to see as they checked into their respective hotels that evening.

Sarah wasn't able to sleep well due to the awkward silence with which John replied to her for expressing her jealousy towards John's wife. Before going to bed, she got a call from the receptionist mentioning that John wanted to talk to her. She rushed down to see John waiting for her at the café, and she indeed joined him there.

John said nothing but smiled. Sarah was very impatient and started to apologize to him for being so naive at noon. He replied with another smile and continued sipping his coffee. Sarah was very unsettled and couldn't say another word in front of him; the impatience started to turn her face red.

After being done with his coffee, John stood up to leave, saying one sentence: "I am not a perfect man; I too have my flaws, like being silent in the most critical situations; it's my wife who turned them into my special character by complimenting them." He continued, "Being jealous of anything that others possess is good if you want to turn that emotion into positive fuel, but if you want exactly what they have, or at least something similar, you are paving a path to hell." He concluded, "Know first what you want, and then it will come to you effortlessly."

Sarah broke into tears upon realizing how foolish she was, not by expressing her emotion of jealousy but by being jealous of something she did not want; she always wanted a partner of some characters that her girlfriends told her about but not what she wanted.

A true mentor may not speak for an hour, but for sure, they speak for a lifetime in seconds.
-Omkara Cheetrala
Indian Author and Speaker

The following day, John made the decision to take David and Sarah on a hike to a lake in the neighborhood. As a result, he called them to their hotels and extended an invitation, which David and Sarah accepted because they wanted to take advantage of the best opportunity to make the most of their trip to this city. The three of them took pleasure in the breathtaking scenery as they walked, and John shared additional details about his path to success with them.

John said that even though he had had many problems and failed at things along the way, he had learned how important it was to keep a positive attitude and keep his mind on his goals. He spoke to them about the power of visualization and how he had used it to help him achieve his goals and overcome the challenges he faced along the way.

When they finally got there, John made the suggestion that they go for a swim in the lake. At first, David and Sarah were both literally and figuratively hesitant about John's advice to take a leap of faith. He advised them that, in order to make progress in certain areas, it is necessary to be willing to take risks and experiment with new things at times.

David and Sarah took John's recommendation and went swimming in the lake, which left them feeling refreshed and re-energized. Following their swim, they sat on the shore, and John's picnic lunch, which he had packed for them, was enjoyed by all of them.

You can control your emotions, not situations:

During their meal, John got a call from his assistant. The assistant told John that there had been a mistake in setting up his appointments. John was supposed to go to a big event that afternoon, but his assistant made a mistake and booked him twice, so he couldn't make it.

The first emotion that came to John's mind was dissatisfaction and frustration. Because this was a fantastic chance for him to broaden the scope of his company, he had been looking forward to this event with great anticipation. However, rather than allowing his feelings to take over, John took a deep breath and reminded himself of the strategies he had learned for maintaining a positive attitude and remaining focused.

He closed his eyes and imagined being at the event, where he would make fruitful connections and grow his company. Even though things weren't going according to plan, he used self-hypnosis to reprogram his subconscious mind to believe that everything was working out in his favor. This helped him feel more optimistic about the situation.

"Your thoughts and feelings are powerful magnets that attract to you the people, circumstances, and events that are in harmony with them. By focusing on what you want and feeling grateful for it, you can attract it into your life."
-Sadhrugu Jaggi Vasudev (1957)
Indian Spiritual Leader

John's ability to stay calm and focused got better over time as he continued to visualize. He was aware that he could not control everything that took place in his life, but he was able to exert control over his own thoughts and feelings.

John decided to make the most of his day after gaining some much-needed illumination and perspective. He then took David and Sarah to a nearby coffee shop, where they ate breakfast and talked about what they had just learned.

By the time the breakfast was over, John had developed a sense of gratitude for the opportunity to put his skills to use and to share those skills with David and Sarah.

The 3 Lessons:

As the three were discussing, John suddenly became aware that David and Sarah had to cancel their return tickets to their respective locations at the last minute to make it to meet John. So, to show his appreciation for the gratitude they had shown him, John called his travel agent and made arrangements for David and Sarah's return trip to be rescheduled so that they would not incur any cancellation fees and any paid shall be refunded immediately. Just before they parted ways, John summarized the three lessons he had taught them:

1. You might not be able to control the circumstances under which you find yourself, but you can control how you react to those circumstances if you choose not to react to them in the first place.

2. There are times when life presents us with opportunities that require us to take a risk in order to reap the full benefits of those opportunities. As the proverb goes, "Give all-you-have with a whatever-it-takes attitude and watch the universe conspire to return more than what-you-need."

3. If you find yourself in a position where you are obligated to help others, you may not always have to pay

the price; all you have to do is find the right person to assist you, like my travel agent, and he winks 😊

He continued by saying, "Even better, let me conclude my three lessons in one line: "You are the creator of your own universe, and so I call it the *YOUniverse*," and wishing the listeners "all the best in your journey to create your abundant *YOUniverse*."

U-Turn:

After their trip with John, David felt encouraged and resolved to make positive changes in his life, and he returned home feeling like he had accomplished a lot. He was well aware of the fact that he needed to lift himself and his family out of the cycle of poverty in which they had been living their entire lives.

David started out by focusing his attention on his objectives and imagining himself successfully completing them. He reprogrammed his subconscious mind through self-hypnosis to believe in his capabilities and harnessed the power of the law of attraction to bring the things he desired into his life.

David finally took the initiative to apply for a job that he had always been interested in but was never able to land. He prepared for the interview by visualizing himself answering all of the questions with ease and enjoying the experience. He used visualization as a form of mental rehearsal.

David experienced feelings of readiness and self-assurance as the day of the interview drew near. He responded without hesitation to all of the questions, and he was able to have a meaningful conversation with the person conducting the interview.

David was taken aback and overjoyed when an offer was immediately made for the job. He was overjoyed at the prospect of working in the job of his dreams and was aware that he had earned this opportunity as a direct result of his perseverance and upbeat attitude.

David worked diligently and maintained his focus on his goals as he started his new job. He stayed optimistic and motivated by applying the strategies that he had learned from John, and before long, he had amassed enough savings to launch a side business in addition to his primary occupation.

"The mind is everything; what you think you become."
-The Buddha (563 BCE -483 BCE)
Spiritual teacher and the founder of Buddhism.

David was able to provide for his family in ways that he had never imagined were possible as the success of his business continued to grow. He was able to provide them with the things they required and make their lives pleasant and secure in spite of their circumstances.

David was thankful that he had the chance to gain knowledge from John and put the strategies that John had taught him to use to make positive changes in his life. He was confident that if he worked hard and kept a positive attitude, he could achieve his objectives and triumph over any challenge that stood in his way. And he couldn't wait to see what the future had in store for him.

David was successful in creating his very own YOUniverse by making use of the tools that he had acquired from John. This YOUniverse was replete with happiness and abundance. He was finally able to fulfil his lifelong goal of achieving the desired level of financial security while also meeting his family's needs. And he was well aware that if he kept putting in the effort required and maintained an optimistic outlook, the sky was the limit for him.

David's nephew was fascinated by his uncle's story from his mother and asked David to tell him more. David smiled and told his nephew about his trip with John and how he had learned the power of positivity and visualization.

As he spoke, David was reminded of Sarah and how she had been struggling with her own challenges. He decided to give her a call and check in on her.

Sarah's story:

When Sarah answered the phone, David immediately sensed that something was off. She appeared to be in a better mood and exuded greater assurance than before. He was concerned about her well-being, so she shared with him the improvements that she had made in her life ever since they had gone on their excursion with John.

After getting divorced, it was difficult for Sarah to move on with her life. She had never been able to control her attraction to the wrong types of men, and as a result, she found herself in a cycle of unhealthy relationships. She had the impression that she was unable to break free of the patterns that were preventing her from progressing.

But after going to that seminar that John was leading and learning about the power of positive thinking and visualization, Sarah started to have a new perspective on the situation. She came to the conclusion that she was the only person who could alter her own life and bring about the kind of romantic connection that she desired.

Sarah, who was resolute in her goal to break free from her past, started working on herself. She concentrated on her own sense of worth and used visualization to picture herself in a relationship with a partner who was loving and supportive. She used self-hypnosis to change her limiting beliefs and the law of attraction to bring more positivity into her life.

Sarah began to attract more than just a simple change as she worked on herself and her own frequency. She began to attract a fantastic business opportunity, as well as an investor who believed in her vision.

It didn't take long for Sarah and her investor to become fast friends, and they quickly got to work building a thriving business together. Their professional lives coincided with the growth and development of their relationship, which culminated in their wedding shortly thereafter.

Sarah and her husband couldn't have been happier to be constructing their lives, both personally and professionally, alongside one another. They were raking in six figures in profits each and every month thanks to the successful operation of their business.

Sarah and her husband made the decision to start a family as the success of their business continued to grow. They were overjoyed to be able to raise a child together and welcomed a beautiful baby into their lives with open arms.

Sarah was able to create the kind of life she had always wanted to live as a result of the tools that she had learned from John, which is another way of saying that Sarah created her own YOUniverse. She was thankful for the chance to learn from John and was aware that anything could be accomplished with enough effort, a positive attitude, and the ability to visualize success. She could hardly wait to see what the future had in store for her and her loved ones.

David and Sarah looked back fondly on their time spent travelling with John and discussed the many ways in which their lives had improved as a result of the experiences they gained on that trip. They were both in agreement that they owed John a significant amount of gratitude for the strategies that he had taught them.

David and Sarah decided to make plans to meet at a local coffee shop that was a favorite of both of them. David and Sarah were sitting down at their favorite café when David recalled how John had taught him the power of positivity and visualization and how he had used these techniques to get his dream job and start his own business. Sarah recalled how John had assisted her in releasing her attachment to her past and attracting the kind of partner she desired.

As they drank the last of their coffee and got ready to part ways, they both felt an overwhelming sense of appreciation for the chance to catch up with one another and talk about the things that had happened in their lives.

It is time to show some gratitude:

As they returned to their vehicles, they couldn't help but reflect on John and the significant role he had played in each of their lives. They made the decision to pay a visit to the location where they had spent the previous two days with him in the hopes of reuniting with him and expressing their gratitude for all that he had done for them.

However, as they got closer to the location, they were confronted with a depressing and unanticipated sight. They noticed a crowd of people congregating and crying, and this tipped them off that something was seriously wrong.

They were shocked and heartbroken to learn that John had passed away a year ago that day and his wife also left the world 3 nights after John's death. They were overcome with grief and unable to comprehend how a man who was so thoughtful, generous, and experienced could no longer be with them.

While David and Sarah stood there paying their respects to John and thinking about everything, he had done for them, they were aware that John's memory would live on in their hearts as well as in the hearts of the people whose lives he had touched. David didn't just improve some people's lives; he also spawned an entire generation of creators who can now make their own YOUniverses filled with joy and prosperity. And this generation would not end here but rather give birth to creators of the YOUniverse.

As they thought about John and everything, he had taught them, they began to cry. Tears streamed down their faces. They experienced profound feelings of loss and sadness, as well as profound feelings of gratitude for the time they had been able to spend with him.

Despite of the fact that he had passed away, John continued to be a significant influence in their lives, motivating them to maintain their forward momentum and make constructive adjustments. They vowed to never forget his teachings and to put the tools he had given them to use so that they could continue to improve not only their own lives but also the lives of those who were close to them.

As David and Sarah were turning to leave the location, they made the proclamation that even though John had passed away from this physical world, he would continue to live on forever in their hearts and in the lives of everyone else whose life he had influenced. They were confident that the legacy he left behind would continue to motivate and encourage people for many years to come.

David and Sarah walked away from the location with heavy hearts and a renewed sense of purpose and determination. They were prepared to continue their own journey and honor John's memory by living their lives to the fullest and doing so to the best of their abilities.

The End.

Summary:

- ❖ You cannot control the situations that happen to you but your emotions, you can.

- ❖ Your response towards an incident speaks a lot about you to your own subconscious and attracts more of such situations.

- ❖ Life is full of opportunities and kind people ready to help, all it takes is a simple plunge to get all-in to win.

- ❖ You don't have to be a "know-it-all" person always, you should know a person who knows it well.

- ❖ Lessons learnt without implementation are like Golden seeds in a dry land.

- ❖ Visualization isn't a technique of projecting a fictitious image but rather working for it and visualizing the effort bearing its fruits.

- ❖ Gratitude attitude takes you to the next level in life.

- ❖ No man will ever stay on this planet forever, do something significant in people's lives, so you can stay in people's hearts forever rent-free.

CHAPTER 2:
WHAT ARE "THE ZEROTH APPLE" AND "THE YOUNIVERSE"?

After reading the first chapter, you might have picked up some interesting life lessons with which I can assure you the value that you invested in this book is paid well. However, I am a fan of under promising and overdelivering results.

Yes, you saw that right, I do not deliver value, I deliver results. If you find someone promising you that they could deliver more value, don't fall for that trap, ask them what are the results? I could build a skyscraper for you but what is results are going to see if that was built in the middle of a desert? Don't fall for Value, ask for Results.

With that being discussed, now let's get into the main topic of discussion: "What?" "What is "The Zeroth Apple?", Why did I name my book something that is SEO poor, not an easy title to Market and Advertise but then Why? Continue to ask more questions, I am not promising you that I would answer them all but you will find the answers yourself soon for sure.

What is "The Zeroth Apple":

The first thought for this book's title was "Nikola Tesla's Secret YOUniverse," and as an SEO expert, I was thinking about keywords and traffic I could attract to my book, but immediately I got my awareness back that this book isn't about how much money I make from the sales of it; my purpose for writing this book is much beyond that.

I want to live forever, like John in our story, in the hearts of the people whom I touched by delivering this concept to their disposal.

That is when my oldest concept came to me. A concept you will understand in the coming paragraphs but before I let you go there, I want to make something clear, although I have a copyright and registered the title of this book, I cannot take any credit for this idea (idea but not title, title is my creativity) because I believe that everything is already in this universe; I just need to vibrate at a certain frequency to tap into it. Just like a radio, the radio is always there, and the frequency is also always there, but only when the radio is tuned properly to that frequency do we stop hearing that static noise and listen to some beautiful conversations or songs.

Similarly, trust me or not, there are many jargons and vocabulary terms that just flickered in my mind without my awareness while I am compiling this manuscript; there are some words that I, myself, cannot recollect now if I wish to quote them but that strangely appear in other chapters of this very book you are reading. It is like, while I was writing that chapter, I was vibrating at such a frequency that the vocabulary came to me; it is not me but the universe through me that is writing this book; I am just a medium.

Now the old idea of mine was, "This world is now in this situation because of three influential apples: Eve-Adam's Apple, Isaac Newton's Apple, and Steve Jobs's Apple, and whatever I am speaking to you right now is beyond them." Well, now, with no pride, I could say, "I discovered but not created something," and yet that is beyond the three influential Apples we ever knew to date.

And hence I named this book title after my personal favorite title, my company "The Zeroth Apple," also referring to the concept as "The Zeroth Apple Concept."

What is "The YOUniverse":

As we go further into the book, we will see the details of why "**The YOUniverse**"? For the time being, the **YOUniverse** wordplay simply means that YOU are the master of your own universe, and thus the two words came together to form the word **YOUniverse**.

So, whenever I mention YOUniverse in this book, it means I am either reminding you that you have the power to manifest whatever you want in your life, and hence you become the master of your universe, which turns out to be **YOUniverse.**

Now, this **YOUniverse** is unique to each person; don't try to find a definition on the internet until this book has sold a million copies worldwide and this word has become a buzzword, or you may fail to find a proper definition.

To be honest with you, I am unsure if this title even works well for this book's marketing and sales because I cannot list any specific keywords to market this well, I don't even have a great background to get sales from my fame, and I am neither a social media giant. Maybe by the time you read this book, I may have 1,000 followers. I am being optimistic here.

But my purpose is never to make a million dollars and become rich from the sales of this book as I already mentioned in the previous chapter; my only desire is that everyone should be able to make the most of their journey in this life by knowing the secret they already possess within them.

To get to the point, the human mind perceives the material world, or 3D reality, as the basis of reality. When we put on a VR headset, we enter a different world and feel like we're walking on it. In the same way, we think that matter and space are the most fundamental parts of the universe and that our consciousness comes from them.

In fact, most secular explanations say that atoms have hit each other, and that's how the first bacteria and other things came to be. This view of the universe is so ingrained in our subconscious minds that it's hard for us to question the reason we're here.

But these are just ideas and thoughts; we think the world out there exists whether or not there is a "me" there. How do we know that, though? If we never experience the world, we only experience a "me" that seems to see a world.

Is it not?

Many people don't care about this question, but you and I do because we want to find the truth and be free of unconscious beliefs. This question is crucial because it turns your attention inward.

This is not a call to reject the material world. Instead, it is a call to create a space within yourself where you can question your ultimate nature, to sit in silence and think about what makes YOU, what is your essence, to go deeper into self-enquiry, to know thyself.

In a dream, for example, the material world seems real, but it's all made up by the mind. You haven't even left your bed, but your mind can trick you into thinking you're falling out of a plane.

This is also backed up by quantum physics and Einstein's theory of relativity, which implies that matter (mass) and energy are interchangeable and that they are different faces of the same mysterious coin.

Can I say that consciousness creates matter or that matter creates consciousness?

Whatever it could be, understand this fundamental concept: we do not have a mind within us; in fact, there is no physical place where the mind is because the mind is not a thing to be placed within your body. The mind is nothing but your thoughts, perceptions, feelings, and emotions.

Our thoughts are in our minds. **"OUR THOUGHTS ARE IN OUR MINDS."** Allow that statement to sink deep into your mind.

I know very well that I spoke about a lot of indigestible concepts in less than 10 paragraphs or half a page so, to help you understand the depth of this rabbit hole, I came up with some theories:

Theory 1: We are living in a dream:

Yes, this sounds like the film *"Inception"* by Christopher Nolan; this man has a special place in my heart. But let me ask you some questions:

1. "When was the last time you had a dream that was so realistic and felt like you weren't dreaming at all but were living a real life?"

2. "If you can experience a dream at such a realistic level, doesn't that mean your brain is a powerful simulator?"

3. "If your brain can simulate such a beautiful, experiential dream, how sure are you that this, right now, is a real experience?"

4. Do you remember anything from your birth?

5. Can you remember any of your childhood days?

6. Do you know anything beyond and apart from what you experienced, you were told, or have heard till now?

If you answered "yes" to any of the above-mentioned last 3 questions, then you should send a note to the Guinness Book of World Records.

If you are just like me, whose answer is a consistent "no", then be my guest to take the never built roller coaster ride with so many humps, bumps and turn arounds going forward through this book one step at a time?

Now let's assume that you are sleeping, and "the real you" wanted a very pleasant, exciting, and positive dream. Can you, have it? Maybe, or maybe not. But you can try, and after a certain number of tries, you will succeed eventually.

From a different perspective, let's say you are already in a dream; you got into awareness, but not entirely, just enough to realize that you are in a dream, and so you can choose to decide what can happen next in that dream. Wouldn't you go for the best choice you have?

That is exactly what I am trying to communicate here with you. Think through and against time; everything that has happened to you thus far is due to the choices you have made for yourself, isn't it? Having a bad day is nothing, but you took some bad decisions yesterday, maybe or an hour ago, even maybe a year ago but for sure it is your choice.

Is it not?

Answer me this: Can you make the right decisions for the next 24 hours and be ready to face any consequences that may come your way?

If you can do that for 24 hours, can you do that for a week?

If you could do that for a week, why not for a month? Why not for a year? Why not for entire life?

So, it is possible that you could choose to decide what you want to do right now, and that would decide your future consequences. That clearly implies that you have the ability to choose what happens to you in the future, excluding the uncontrollable variables in the long run. Why can't you do it in the short term if you can do it in the long run?

Isn't it true that you have control over what happens to you in 5 years? If you can control your five-year futuristic destination, what about three years from now?

What about 1 year from now? You can choose what happens in your life in a year if you make the right decisions.

If you can make a decision for something a year in the future, you can do the same for yourself one month from now.

Similarly, you can control situations that occur to you in a week's time. If you can control the consequences of your life that you may face a week from now, you can also choose what your life should be a day from now.

If you can create your life for one day, you could create your own YOUniverse for the next moment.

Consider this now: You are reading this line because you decided to read this word; you decided to continue reading because YOU decided to do so; and you are still reading because YOU decided to do so. You may not know who I am; you may not even have heard of me to date; you do not even know that I exist, possibly, but you are reading this because you decided to, not because I wrote it.

So, I have no say in whether or not you read this book; you have complete control over what you want and do. This level of clarity and detail gives me the authority to present my first proposal:

We are living in a dream which is under our own control. You get to choose what can happen next to you in your life and that is called Manifestation.
-Omkara Cheetrala
Indian Author and Speaker

Theory 2: We are part of a simulation:

We can all use computers today, which can be used to make digital worlds. Computers have changed so much in recent years that we can now create artificial intelligence that can think for itself.

To go even further, an AI can make another AI or a copy of itself in the world we made.

Now that the AI we created can make a computer with which it could possibly create the world and still think it has created the world inside a computer that is created, but we are the masters who made that AI in the first place.

Is it or not? Now, isn't that true for all of us?

We can create an AI and think that we are creating that AI, but possibly we are playing within the world created and being simulated by someone above and beyond us.

I propose that we are all trying to mutate inside a simulation, trying to create our own worlds within the world that are created as a test environment by someone outside and beyond this world.

To generalize, some call them God, while I call them the universe.

Consider this now: We previously understood that we are humans who work within the Time, Space, and Matter continuum. If someone has to define God, they will probably say something like: God is someone who is outside, beyond, and who can control and is not affected by this Time, Space, and Matter continuum.

Let's take this debate further: Will we ever be able to look after every creature within that simulation that we created? Probably not after it reached a certain population, but surely, we can focus on those that are raising red flags and giving us warning signals. Does that sound familiar to you, *"The Prayers"*?

To avoid too much of that work, imagine that we gave the simulation enough power to create its own YOUniverse as per its wishes without causing damage to the creation we made in the first place. I think this is exactly what's happening to us right now.

Look at any statistics right now. Earlier, the deaths were too many, not many millionaires and billionaires were like rare stars, and even after a lot of hard work, not everyone would get what they wanted. But today? Today, everything is at our fingertips.

People call it evolution, and I agree with them, but evolution also gives us control over ourselves. We have mutated and populated this universe enough that the creator of this universe has given us the power to manifest our own YOUniverse.

In the history of mankind, this is the right time for all of us to make the best out of it, this time, this century, this lifetime is the time we could make miracles happen in our lives.

My proposal with this theory is: If you have watched the film "*The Matrix*," I will be your Morpheus, Neo! You are the one. You are "THE ONE," and we are all living in the matrix, which is partially under our own control until we live within it without trying to destroy it.

The question never was, "Is it possible?" it was always, "Are you ready to make it possible?"
-Omkara Cheetrala
Indian Author and Speaker

Theory 3: Aham Brahmasmi:

This is actually not a theory but a Sanskrit mantra from the Advaita Tradition, which loosely translates to "I am the Creator." This is, in fact, the fourth and final Principle of Mahavakya:

Prajnanam Brahma: Consciousness is Brahman

Ayam Atma Brahma: This self is Brahman.

Tat Tvam Asi: "Thou art that" or "You are one"

Aham Brahmasmi: I am Brahman, or I am Divine.

There was also an Indian-originated historical Hindu story that supports my earlier proposals, which, loosely translated to English, would be like this:

Once upon a time, at the beginning of time, there was the creator god Brahma. He was the one responsible for creating the universe and everything that existed within it. But even with all the power and knowledge at his disposal, Brahma could not shake off the feeling of boredom and emptiness. He longed for something more, something to entertain himself with. So, he thought of creating Maya, the force of illusion, as a way to play a game.

Maya, once created, was a beautiful and captivating being with the power to shape and manipulate reality. She said to Brahma, "Let's play the most interesting game ever!" and Brahma, excited by the proposal, agreed. Without knowing the consequences, Brahma started playing this game with Maya, using the power of illusion to shape the world as we know it today. He created mountains and oceans, animals, and plants. Brahma was still feeling incomplete, and as per Maya's suggestion, he even created humans.

The game interested Brahma, and as they continued playing, Brahma found himself getting lost in the illusions that Maya had created. He became so entranced by the beauty and complexity of the world that he had created that he started to lose sight of reality. Sensing Brahma's vulnerability, Maya took advantage and broke him into pieces, scattering him across the universe. Each piece of Brahma was placed within the heart of every being, making them all a part of the creator god himself.

Brahma, now shattered, watched as his creations continued to live out their lives, unaware of the true nature of their existence. He felt deep sadness and regret for what he had done and for getting lost in the illusions that he had created. He realized that his game with Maya had turned into a trap and had caused him to lose his true self. He understood that the game of Maya is not just a game; it's the game of life, and its illusions are the ones that make it interesting.

This story serves as a reminder that we are the Brahma within and that we have the power to shape our future and destiny. We are not just mere mortals but creators in our own right. It's up to us to use this power wisely, to shape our reality, and to be aware of the illusions that may try to deceive us. It's up to us to create our own story and to make it an interesting one.

With this story being told, **I would like to make another proposal:** we are living Brahmas in our own creation, and it is just a matter of time before we realize that so we could create our own YOUniverse.

I don't know who God really is but all that I know is, we are surely a part of him in power, in control, in the heart.
-Omkara Cheetrala
Indian Author and Speaker

Theory 3: You are the YOUniverse.

This is a concept where, without you, there is nothing that exists. This sounds very naive and senseless, but hold my hand tight and just follow me, help me help you to learn how deep this rabbit hole goes.

Let me ask you, "How did you like the book so far?" Your answer could be that it is good, could be better, or something else.

Now I would ask the same question to my nephew, who cannot read yet but could speak; what would his response be? "I don't know."

For him, this book doesn't even interest him; he even doesn't care for the book. Of course, this book materialistically exists here in your hands right now, maybe in digital or printed format; it doesn't matter, but it exists. Will the fact that this book exists make any difference to my nephew, who has never read it?

No, because he cannot read it.

Similarly, if I take a blind person to shopping and asked how does this appear to them? His response would be, "How will I know?" Even if he cares, he cannot see the color, so it does not matter to him. All that matters to him is some piece of cloth that covers his body and fits it properly.

Similarly, people with Anosmia, who lost their sense of smell, can't care for the smell, and people with Ageusia, who lost their taste buds, can't care for the taste.

Well, let's take this to the next level by adding you to the equation. If I ask you, how was the dinner last night? "It tasted good, delicious, colorful, flavorful, and fragrant," you would say, "it watered your mouth," and so on.

If I may ask you, "How was the dinner last night?" But only this time, answer me without adding any information related to your senses. How would you describe it?

You cannot.

Because some food exists only so you had it—the taste exists because your tongue tasted it, the smell exists because your nose detected it, and the food exists because you saw it. What happened to your dinner is exactly what happens to the whole universe.

It doesn't matter if there is a gigantic star collapsing in the Milky Way if you cannot see it, or if a comet is crossing the Earth's orbit if it doesn't disturb you; nothing matters if you aren't there or if you aren't ready to care for it.

"Without the observer, there is nothing."
-Omkara Cheetrala
Indian Author and Speaker

Now, tell me, without your seeking abundance, is there any abundance? Without you trying to be rich, is there still richness? Is there peace in your life if you are not looking for it?

Materialistically, all of them exist, just like this book, but it doesn't matter to you unless you care for it. When you care about something, you add emotion and feeling to it.

Conclusion:

With all that being said and written, I request that you kindly understand that I am not the father of this concept; it is just like Newton's Laws of Gravity. Do you think only on that day the apple fell off a tree and hit Sir Isaac Newton? No, every day, tens, if not hundreds, of apples fall from trees after being ripped.

But because someone was curious enough to ask "Why" and "How," the rest is history. Similarly, this is like gravity: it existed, is still existing, and will continue to exist indefinitely.

This concept honestly predates me, you, and everyone who could read this book practically.

Well, when there are new concepts that are introduced into society, there will always be some misconceptions, which I would like to address a few of but not all of, but these would be enough for you to move ahead and complete this book.

Trust me, if you read this book carefully, you'll be a master of this idea by the time you're done. You might even be able to write a whole book about the mistakes you might make with your new knowledge, which then turns into wisdom.

Summary:

- I believe that three apples transformed the world into what we see today and that "*The Zeroth Apple*" concept existed before all of these and was thus named as such.

- You are the master of your universe, and so wherever appropriate, it was mentioned as **YOUniverse**.

- We are all living in a dream, which we have control over; we can choose what we want to happen to us in the future.

- We are part of a simulation in which we have been given semi-control over everything without destroying this creation.

- Aham Brahmasmi, I am the creator, The God as per Hindu mythological Indian Originated story about Brahma and Maya.

- We are in the best time of history to make the best of our lives.

CHAPTER 3:
USUAL MYTHS AROUND THIS CONCEPT?

The Law of Attraction, The Law of Manifestation and The Zeroth Apple concept are all same:

The Law of Attraction and the Law of Manifestation are often used interchangeably, but they are similar but not exactly the same thing.

The Law of Attraction is based on the idea that like energy attracts like energy and that by focusing on positive thoughts and emotions, we can attract positive experiences and outcomes into our lives. This is often associated with the idea that we can manifest our desires through the power of our thoughts and feelings.

The Law of Manifestation, on the other hand, refers to the idea that we can manifest or bring into reality whatever we desire through the power of our thoughts, intentions, and actions. This idea is based on the belief that we can change our reality with the power of our minds and that we can create abundance, success, and happiness by focusing our thoughts and energy on what we want to create.

Both the Law of Attraction and the Law of Manifestation say that our thoughts and beliefs can change our reality. However, the Law of Manifestation says that we can actively bring about what we want through our thoughts and actions, while the Law of Attraction focuses more on the power of positive thoughts and emotions to bring about positive experiences.

Coming to "The Zeroth Apple" concept is closely related to "The Law of Manifestation." However, on top of using the power of our minds, we reinforce the power with the support of other techniques that we are going to cover in the following chapters.

It is important to remember that none of these theories or practices has been proven by science. For example, there's no scientific evidence that just thinking positively will make things happen or change reality.

However, "The Zeroth Apple" concept shares the credentials of the techniques that were scientifically backed, and hence this cannot be treated entirely as an occult science.

This New concept is another occult science just like Reiki Healing, Aura Healing, and Qigong:

Anyone who understands the basic human sciences and an atom's topology would agree to this: we living beings are made of cells that were made of atoms, which in turn are composed of a nucleus (protons and neutrons) and electrons revolving and rotating simultaneously.

Also, human science says that every healthy, complete human is made of 35 billion cells. Before I get into the myth, let me tell you something: Sir Isaac Newton, A. P. J. Abdul Kalam, Nikola Tesla, Albert Einstein, you, and I are all made of the same number of 35 billion cells. We all have the same hardware; it is just the software that is different for each of us.

Nevertheless, scientists also claimed that each cell possesses a minimum of 0.07 millivolts, which is a very tiny charge. But when we multiply that by the number of cells we are made of:

0.07 millivolts X 35 billion cells

= 2.45 billion millivolts = 2.45 Gigavolts

Did you notice the units? It was not a million but a billion (a Giga is a billion) volts; in other words, we are a walking nuclear reactor explosion. This energy is exactly what we are trying to control via the Mudras, the Aura, Reiki, Chi in Qigong, and now this new technique.

When something has an electric charge, it is bound to have a magnetic charge or field (is the more technical term), Well! I won't go into details neither this is a science textbook, but please review Induced Electromotive Force or Back Electromotive Force (EMF), The Pauli Exclusion Principle, Heisenberg's Uncertainty Principle, and Lenz's Law of Current.

Collectively, the above laws indicate that the electron within the cells has charge and spin, which produce current and induce magnetic fields, and on top of all these, everything is literally vibrating. Yes, what you see right now with your eyes looks solid, feels solid, and even sounds solid, but they are not solid at the atomic level; they are vibrating.

Dr B. M. Hedge quotes, Nobel laureate in Quantum Physics Hans Peter Duerr (Dürr)'s article titled, "**Matter is not made out of matter,**" and he calls the essence of the complete work in simple terms, "Aduality," which means there is no duality that exists, there is no matter and energy in separation, they are like 2 sides of the same coin.

And in the same speech, the doctor continued and quoted some important points mentioned in Mr. Duerr's work, where Mr. Duerr took a reference from "**Kṣhetra Kṣhetrajña Vibhāg Yog (13.16).**" What he mentioned was enlightening, and let me elaborate on that:

बहिरन्तश्च भूतानामचरं चरमेव च |
सूक्ष्मत्वात्तदविज्ञेयं दूरस्थं चान्तिके च तत् | |

bahir antaśh cha bhūtānām acharaṁ charam eva cha
sūkshmatvāt tad avijñeyaṁ dūra-sthaṁ chāntike cha tat
-Kṣhetra Kṣhetrajña Vibhāg Yog (13.16)
Upanishad

The concept of Advaita Vedanta (or Advaitham) is a Vedic doctrine that identifies the individual self (atman) with the ground of reality (brahman). It is associated primarily with the Indian philosopher Shankara, famously referred to as Shankaracharya (exact dates are unknown but somewhere close to c. 700–c. 750 CE).

The above Sanskrit sloka translates to:

bahir antaśh cha bhūtānām: It is inside and outside of everything.

acharaṁ charam eva cha: It moves all the time but looks very solid.

sūkṣhmatvāt tad avijñeyaṁ: It is so subtle that no science/ knowledge can see nor explain it.

dūra-sthaṁ chāntike cha tat: It is extremely far away at the same time, very close and near.

To summarize, "It is inside and outside of everything, constantly moving or vibrating but appearing very solid." "It is so subtle that no science could prove it, and no one with any knowledge can see it or explain it." "While it is very far, at the same time, it is very close and near."

The doctor also states that this is the exact description of an electron and atoms. So, after a lot of research, it has been concluded that every atom present in each cell of our body is vibrating in synchrony. Now the word "synchrony" is the key here.

Synchrony with what?

We all know that Earth revolves around the sun at a certain speed and on a particular orbit because that is the orbit where the pulling force of the gigantic star called the Solar System's Sun and the repelling force of the only known life-hosting planet, Earth, nullify each other. As is the case with other planets, they cling to life rather than collapsing like comets or asteroids.

Similarly, to keep all these vibrating cells both in synchrony and from jumping into somebody's body, there must be something acting on them!

And that is the mind, thoughts, feelings, and emotions we have. We are a colony of thirty-five billion cells that are in synchrony with each other and with our thoughts. This takes us to the next myth.

If you want to find the secrets of the Universe,
Think in terms of Energy, Frequency and Vibration
-Nikola Tesla (1856-1943)
Serbia American Inventor

Law of Attraction, Affirmations, Self-Hypnosis, Auto Suggestion, NLP, and Ho'oponopono and this new concept are nothing but time waste:

When you are in sync with your own thoughts, beliefs, and frequencies amalgamated with emotions, as we understood from our last myth, you would obviously understand and agree now that if we could alter them, we could alter the vibrations and energy states of the cells and, in turn, the universe, as the Advaith Vedanta states, "बहिरन्तश्च भूतानाम्" "bahir antaśh cha bhūtānām" it is outside and inside of everything and everywhere.

We all know why soldiers break their march every three steps when crossing a bridge; we all know that a stampede of 100 people on a hanging bridge could collapse if the stampede matches the natural frequency of the bridge. Now I'm saying the same thing, but on a tiny scale where you can't see everything.

You too, can resonate with a new thought, emotion, frequency, and belief system that could resonate with the universe, conspiring everything to make your desire fall into place as you wish. And that is called "manifesting the YOUniverse."

But anything requires guidance, guidelines, and a set of instructions if we are expecting a desired outcome, and so researchers, doctors, and experts finally decided on some practices that work for them under their traditions and cultures.

That's where the Law of Attraction comes in: thinking positively, using affirmations to speak out loud what we want, and using self-hypnosis to awaken our subconscious mind in order to change our habits and behaviors.

The Ho'oponopono method, in which we seek forgiveness, love, and love more of this place, and vibrate at higher positive frequencies.

The NLP technique of speaking to our own brain in its own language so we could automatically feel and vibrate in a certain way; and using all of these to our benefit to manifest our own YOUniverse—this is all about this new YOUniverse.

Maybe we do not have, right now, major scientific experimental proofs, but that is the same case with the heliocentric theory. Until a telescope was discovered, the wise men who claimed that Earth was not the center of the solar system and proposed an anti-geocentric theory were executed. The best example is the Polish astronomer Nicolaus Copernicus in the 16th century. Nobody believed in it until it was later expanded and refined by other scientists such as Galileo Galilei, Johannes Kepler, and Isaac Newton, who provided observational and experimental evidence to back it up; however, this does not mean that truth can be hidden forever.

"Everything is energy. And that's all there is to it. Match the frequency of the reality you want, and you cannot help but get that reality. It can be no other way. This is not philosophy. This is physics."

The same is true for our concept of **"The Zeroth Apple"** as it is for manifesting your YOUniverse. We are currently lacking in scientific evidence and proof, but this will surely change soon. Until then, don't blindly believe me; be resentful, skeptical, and critical, but use logic. For me, who is a pessimist in many ways, the logical explanations provided thus far make a lot of logical sense, and I hope you are convinced enough to continue reading this book.

Summary:

- ❖ The Law of Attraction, the Law of Manifestation, and the Zeroth Apple concept all sound the same, but they are not.

- ❖ We are a walking nuclear reactor considering the energy we possess within our cells; controlling it is what we do in Reiki, Aura Healing, Qigong, and the "Zeroth Apple" concept.

- ❖ Everything is vibrating at an atomic level.

- ❖ Our body is a colony of 35 billion atomic cells collectively possessing energy, equivalent to a Nuclear Reactor Explosion.

- ❖ Our cells are in synchrony with our thoughts and emotions.

The Law of Attraction, Ho'oponopono, NLP, affirmations, and "The Zeroth Apple" concept are all wand-like tools that help us control and manifest our desired YOUniverses into reality.

PART TWO: WHAT, WHERE, WHO, WHEN, WHY, AND WHICH?

CHAPTER 4:
WHY, WHEN, WHO, WHICH, WHERE AND WHAT

Why even consider Abundance in life?

I used to have this misconception myself. I wanted to lead a minimalist life; I have everything I want in my life, and I am happy with what I have. I have the capacity to do whatever I want and wish to, but in the end, does it all matter? If I am not going to take anything with me, why do I need abundance?

Why earn more? Why work harder every day? Why should I even work? When would I live the monastic life?

Why am I here in this materialistic world?

I used to wander a lot with these thoughts, and one day I decided to do something about it. I quickly remembered a strange meditation practice not at all close to my home, which was exactly what I wanted and was thinking of: leading the life of a monk.

Yes, the meditation center takes care of accommodation, food, and the basic needs of electricity. It also educates you about the oldest meditation technique that Buddha himself discovered and preached across the nation and outside the nation.

All this for an exchange of no form of money whatsoever, but the catch is "no communication," "live a life of a monk," and "completely Sattvic food." (*A Sattvic diet is a diet based on foods that contain one of the three yogic qualities known as sattva. In this system of dietary classification, foods that decrease the body's energy are considered tamasic, while those that increase the body's energy are considered rajasic.*) only', 'take a plate and glass and stand in a queue to seek food donated by past batches.'

Yes, you get to practice the extraordinary form of meditation for 10 days with the 5 precepts given to you on Day 0. To know more about this technique, I'd encourage you to go to the Vipassana website and invest some decent quality time into it; it is worth every second of your time. This is exactly what I wanted to be: a monk who has no entanglements with the materialistic world and lives happily.

After the mediation practice is done, on the 10th day, the last day of our practice, before we disperse, we are allowed to collect our belongings, which we deposited while entering the camp. We are also told that if you wish to share this practice with the next batch of students, donate whatever you can. Nobody will ask you to pay such an amount, and even if you don't, everybody will be happy with that.

On that day, after the donation drive was done (by the way, I did not donate at all as I wanted to go back with a serious monk feeling but not the same egoistic feeling that I paid for what I got), I bumped into a person who started explaining the history of that place and the practices being shared.

Then he also quoted about a person who donated all that land to Guru ji so he could contribute to his nation's enlightenment. The same day, Guru ji also says something phenomenal in his discourse, which loosely translates to this: "I have all the riches in my life that I could ever experience, and then I came across this technique; had I not been that rich, I would have, for sure, had thoughts to myself about coming back to this practice after becoming rich." I may have also thought that this was for those who are already rich and trying to make more money. But today, I know the fact: it is not for the rich or for the poor; this is for all of those who seek enlightenment in life.

That hit me so hard. Money is energy, which could be used to either fuel my own boat to reach the destination quickly on my own or to pull other people's boats with me to reach the destination steadily.

We can't blame the knife that killed a person; it has nothing to do with the act; it did what it was supposed to do, and so the rest is in the hands of the person who is holding it. The same applies exactly to money too. By holding it, you could try to help others or lead a luxurious life. Please understand that I am not saying that living a luxurious life is bad or selfish; it is necessary for some and perhaps not for others.

After immediately coming back to my residence, I read another quote saying, "You could give only what you have." Wait a minute, that is too deep. The intent of that quote was to refer to your emotion, but the situation and the lenses I have gained from the meditation have helped me look into it deeper.

I wanted to give prosperity to others while I am not striving enough to create prosperity in my own life. If I do not work for my own prosperity, I will not be in a state of giving but end up in a state of seeking.

If I end up being mediocre, all I can give is mediocrity. Thanks to my YOUniverse, soon after this incident I had a teetotaler friend whose father was reported to have jaundice fever. He had no money to even visit his family, so he was sitting there and just trying to control his emotions.

What I could immediately do was give him some money that I could dispose of and never ask him for it again. But not so far, I had to learn that his father had been diagnosed with pancreatic cancer rather than a simple fever. I wish I had more money to help my friend with his father's treatment, but that month, I had to live on credit and spend very carefully, even for my groceries, because I had contributed to my friend's father's treatment.

That whole month, I was very low, not because I gave the money but because I couldn't do anymore, not just for his father but for even the street beggars, the homeless guys that month. This isn't what I wanted in my life. I was seeking mediocrity, and so I was only able to provide mediocre support to my friend. He may not say or think that, but on my part, that was an incomplete help.

Soon after that, I heard another wise man speak on TV about investments and say this: "I heard a lot of losers say that money can't buy happiness." But let me tell you, when your daughter wanted a costly gift and you could afford it without looking at the price tag, isn't that happiness? If your parents are in the hospital, and you gave the doctors assurance that you could bear whatever the price is for the operation, isn't that happiness? People who cannot make a living tell half-baked stories to justify their situation."

That is true, isn't it? Money certainly may not buy us sleep, but it could give us the power to buy a mattress for the homeless which could definitely give us a peaceful night.

Money may not buy peace, but it could have certainly saved the majority of the divorces that were reported to have financial instability as the leading cause.

At the end of the day, God may not ask you how much you earned, but what if he asked, "Why did you not live a life of full potential?" I will not be able to face him. So, I resolved to achieve abundance in all aspects of my life.

The idea of "**The Zeroth Apple**" for creating an abundant **YOUniverse** has helped me improve my spirituality, health, wealth, parenting, career, business, and relationships.

Why should someone trust this technique?

A very valid point to ask; if I were you, I would have asked this long ago, even before I purchased this book.

Do not trust me; will you trust '**The Bhagavad-Gita**'? '**The Upanishad**'? '**The Bible**'?

What about '**The Qur'an**'?

If not, **"The Buddha and his teachings"**?

Or if you are an atheist, will you believe in Napoleon Hill? Benjamin Franklin? Ralph Waldo Emerson Abraham Lincoln? John Muir? Russell H. Conwell? Nikola Tesla? Wallace D. Wattles? William Walker Atkinson James Allen? David O. McKay? Eleanor Roosevelt? Dale Carnegie? Dr Joseph Murphy Norman

Vincent Peale? C.S. Lewis? Maxwell Maltz? Victor Frankl? Peter Drucker? Earl Nightingale? Louise L. Hay? David J. Schwartz? Wayne Dyer?

If you believe any one of them, believe them, not me.

You can get my other book, once published, in which I covered all these references I mentioned above and spoke about the power of how we can manifest our own **YOUniverse.**

"The universe is a vast electric field, and we are all
an integral part of it."
-Nikola Tesla (1856-1943)
Serbia American Inventor

I may be some nobody, but what about all those above-mentioned gods, demi-gods, deities, literature scholars, politicians, scientists, authors, ministers, and people from almost all walks of life who were successful in their fields? You can trust them, right? Then let it be trust them. I am not here to win your trust; I am here to give you the most powerful tool with which you can change your life, and that is more than what I could achieve in this life.

When is the perfect age to manifest YOUniverse?

Anyone under the age of seven is ideal for practicing this technique, **"The Zeroth Apple"—manifesting your YOUniverse**. The next best time is now.

But why is that 7 a cut-off? Well.! Let us talk about that a little more. Say you have been with your family on a week's trip to Bali and sat with me after your return; what will you discuss more in our conversations? about your trip.

Say you have been on that trip for a month. You will have a lot to say and will surely consume more time speaking about that trip.

Say you have been on a trip for a lifetime and have come back to this life. What will you try to communicate more about? Your last trip and you shall have enough experiences to share that would ideally take 7 years of your life through gestures, behaviors, and responses.

This number 7, as I recall, lacks scientific proof, but it is more convincing because, only by that time, we become more aware of our surroundings; until that time, we have a lot of imaginary thoughts; we could ride a unicorn even if we have never seen one in real life. We can jump on lava inside our room from couch to chair.

Below 7 is the age when kids are in Theta mind state, which is nothing but a hypnotic state where your sub-conscious is still open and ready to intake whatever you feed it. After that age, your sub-conscious mind's capacity is full and conscious mind starts kicking-in, making rational decisions, seeking logical explanations, asking questions and finding answers.

We tend to lose our ability to imagine and connect with past lives after the age of seven. For example, disregard the number: after a certain age, we begin to collect information from our surroundings and behave in synchrony with them, and we cease any further display of past behaviors because we have enough time to top-up our subconscious with current life experiences.

Some great thought leaders call this paradigm: you are tuned to the surroundings you belong to. It is exceedingly rare for a slum kid to think of becoming an astronaut after the age of 7, though he always wanted to become one till then. He must have heard that it isn't easy or even possible for them to dream that big.

If you only knew the magnificence of the 3, 6 and 9, then you would have a key to the universe
-Nikola Tesla (1856-1943)
Serbia American Inventor

This is known as paradigmatic or subconscious programming. Once that is established, it becomes increasingly powerful, making it even more challenging to encourage an adult to dream big and tell him about the possibilities he or she could have if they only thought about them.

However, just because you can't go back in time doesn't mean you can't use the concept of **"The Zeroth Apple" – Manifest your YOUniverse.** You could, for sure, but that requires a lot of persistence and patience.

If necessary, we can erase your previous programming and completely rewrite it. If you remember, when I was talking about the myths, I said that we are all made of the same hardware and that the software is what makes a difference. This is what I was talking about.

I am well known for dotting a hazy picture first and then slowly connecting them all one by one so you can have that "Aha!" moment.

This rework on your internal coding requires persistence because your own mind has tried to conflict with the new ideas, we try to put in. Imagine the same kid reaching the age of 18 and working in a local municipality as a day laborer; I tell him he could still be an astronaut today. You might not be able to join the government's space missions, but you could start your own company to invade space. Opportunities abound, but he couldn't see them because he needed a paradigm shift, not just a simple thought.

To make that happen, we must work with him day in and day out, with patience, and first allow him to believe that it is possible; he can dream of it, he can begin working towards it, and eventually, he will have everything he desired.

This is the case with you; if you are reading this book because your relationship isn't going well with your current partner and you want to manifest the best YOUniverse, maybe your value system is conflicting.

This requires a lot of work on your subconscious habits and patterns, which requires patience and consistency. If you are stubborn, you could, for sure, become that next diamond in the mud. It is all dependent on your desire's attachment to you and how strong you are to make that desire a reality. This is what Napoleon Hill refers to as "Burning Desire" in his book, 'Think and Grow Rich'.

Who can practice this technique?

The Zeroth Apple concept of manifesting your desired YOUniverse is just like the law of gravitational attraction in the laws of the universe. Even if you scream out loud, "I don't believe in you, Gravity," and jump off a 7th-floor terrace, you will still be pulled down.

Now, if I ask you, who can experience the pull of gravity? Well, everyone on this planet, for now. Similarly, **"The Zeroth Apple"** concept can be practiced by anyone.

The only criteria are that you follow the rules stated in the following chapters. If you really want to make this the best, you should pay attention to the last two chapters.

By the way, the best part of this concept is that there are no side effects and no investments required. It is all about you and your thought process in correlation with other techniques to make it work quickly for you.

Which part of the day is best to practice?

In terms of the time of day, I would ideally prefer only two times per day. The first hour and the last hour were treated as the **"GOLDEN HOURS."**

In the morning golden hour, you are not totally awake; your subconscious is still active at the same time, and your analytical brain is also active, and that state of mind is referred to as "*The Theta State of mind*".

So, you don't have to go into any trans-type of mental state to work with self-hypnosis or work hard to imprint a new behavior inside your head.

In the night's golden hour, you are literally teaching your brain some thoughts and feelings; dreams occur based on the last thoughts you had, just like the tune you are humming just now sticks with you more than the song in full you heard an hour ago.

This connects your brain neurons in a particular way to reprogram your brain when you are at rest, which means your brain is in its best rest state; there is nothing extra it has to process, and there is nothing to majorly worry about commanding any of the body parts during this time.

A well-established mind is like a Kalpavruksh
-Sadhrugu Jaggi Vasudev
Indian Spiritual Leader

Did you notice that I haven't mentioned a special geographical time? That is because we are talking about your **YOUniverse**, and your biological cycle defines your day; it defines when and how much sleep you need. There are some amazingly productive night owls, and at the same time, there are some artistic people who are early birds. It is all depending on their paradigm and the vibrations their cells are resonating at.

Though everyone's biological cycles are different, practising this technique in the early morning hours is always best to reap the most benefits. Those who could practice this while exposed to the first rays of the sun would be able to master the art of visualization, which in turn speeds up the process of manifestation.

Of course, this is just a prescription, but if you wish to change your own biological cycle to match it with your choice, which is also possible for you with the support of your knowledge about **"The Zeroth Apple"– Manifesting your YOUniverse.**

Where can one practice this technique?

There is no specific place, time, or day for practicing this technique; however, if you want to see faster results in your life, I'd recommend dedicating a place for your practice; this is not to turn you into some kind of devotee, but science has proven that places hold energy.

Have you ever been in a situation where you were comfortable sleeping in a room in a particular spot, but if you make changes to that spot, room, or anything in it, you feel some discomfort and it takes time for you to get the sleep that night? It is because your energy was in sync with the place and the objects within it.

When a change is made to a place, the natural frequency of that place is altered, pushing you to vibrate at trial-and-error frequencies continuously until you find the resonance frequency of the new room. Though it is the same old room, it has a new frequency because of the change we made to it, it shall be referred as a new room as per its new frequency.

Similarly, if you wish to manifest your desired goals within a short period, try to practice this technique in the same place every day and every time you want to practice because that accumulates the energy in that place and makes you feel energized even if you sit in that place with half the intention to practice this technique.

Even better is to practice this technique in groups. Groups raise vibrations and frequencies to higher states. If you find a group of like-minded people in your circle and read this book together and practice this technique together, you will feel a completely different level of energy.

The first and best suggestion would be a holy place of your choice. Especially if that place includes sunlight and water ponds, it is even better. A holy place is where people always try to be in submissive mode, in their most vulnerable state of mind, trying to serve, be calm, and be in seeking mode, always being positive and seeking.

Having such energies around will help you improve your vibrations and frequencies to reach the highest states which could elevate your chances of manifesting your desires the fastest.

What is the typical turnaround time for results?

With the "Where" part being read, this is the perfect time for us to talk about the "What" part of this concept. As I just said in the previous section, the durations are controlled by various factors. Factors like surroundings, group, place, time, state of mind, and much more.

I have students who master this technique in weeks, others who take months, and a few more like myself who took years of hard work without a guru to do everything on their own.

I personally observed that people who practice the technique in groups, along with a guru, immediately after they wake up to a compliment from their loved ones during the early morning hours have the fastest turnaround time to see best results.

It also depends on your desired outcome. If you wish to be healthy when you are forty, it cannot happen tomorrow on your 30th birthday.

If you wish to retire with surplus cash in your account to enjoy your life, it cannot happen tonight by winning that lottery you purchased a week ago.

There are also some rules that you should follow while practicing **"The Zeroth Apple,"** which will be covered in the following chapters. This is why we advise our readers not to discuss this concept with anyone until they have finished reading this book at least once in the fullest. In fact, it is so important not to speak about **"The Zeroth Apple"** concept that I wrote a section on why not to in this book at the end.

At the end of the day, the turnaround time is determined by how desirable you find your goal and a variety of other controllable factors, which you will discover by the end of this book.

Subscribe to my Author Page on Amazon so you shall be informed about the coming parts of this 7 books series inside, from which I will be revealing the secrets of **'The Zeroth Apple'** exclusively for each area of life in detail.

You can reach me at OmkaraCheerala.com or Google Omkara Cheetrala.

Summary:

❖ Abundance is not a choice; it is our moral responsibility towards our society, country, and humankind.

❖ There is no particular time to practice this technique, for best results, the Golden Hour would surely quicken the process.

❖ If a group must fix a time and practice this technique, the best choice would be early in the morning.

❖ The turnaround speed of this technique's results is controlled by variables like state of mind, frequency, group, place, and many other controllable variables.

❖ There is no recommended location, but if one must practice in a group, a holy place with sunlight and a water pond is highly recommended.

❖ "Your destiny is in your own very hands.

❖ It makes no difference whether you are in debt or not; you can seek wealth or health using this technique.

CHAPTER 5:
WHAT ALTERNATE MEDICINE SAYS ABOUT "THE ZEROTH APPLE"!

I'm going to draw inspiration from a variety of techniques that are widely used around the world in various traditional ways and at various levels.

It's important to remember that these healing methods are considered alternative or complementary therapies. Most of them have not been scientifically proven or widely accepted by the mainstream medical community, so they shouldn't be used instead of traditional medical treatment.

"There is no energy in matter other than that received from the environment."
-Nikola Tesla (1856-1943)
Serbia American Inventor

Before I even get into the detailed explanations of the techniques, I would like to briefly introduce each technique in a few lines, so you aren't missing out on the deepest concepts of my following teachings.

Kindly note that these descriptions aren't the exclusive "Out Of The Book" definitions but more of a simple, easy-to-understand one-liner definition for the comfort of the reader, you.

Alternative Techniques quoted across this book:

Aura healing:

It is based on the idea that the body has a subtle energy field called prana and that illness and injury can result from a disruption or imbalance in this energy field.

Practitioners of aura healing believe that this energy field can become damaged or blocked, leading to physical and emotional problems. They work to clear and balance the aura to promote healing and well-being.

Pranic Healing:

It is based on the idea that the body has a subtle energy field called prana just like in the case of Aura and that illness and injury can result from a disruption or imbalance in this energy field.

Practitioners of Pranic healing use techniques such as energy visualization, meditation, and gentle touch to manipulate this energy field in order to promote healing and balance.

Quantum Healing:

It is based on the principles of quantum physics, and practitioners believe that physical reality is created by our thoughts, beliefs, and emotions.

They work to change a person's thoughts, beliefs, and emotions in order to change the physical reality and bring healing.

Somatic Experience:

It is a type of therapy that focuses on the connection between the mind and the body.

It uses techniques such as movement and touches to help individuals become aware of and release stored emotional and physical tension.

Law of Attraction:

This is a philosophy and practice that states that we can manifest our desires into reality by focusing on positive thoughts and feelings.

It's based on the idea that like energy attracts like energy, and that by focusing on positive thoughts and emotions, we can attract positive experiences and outcomes into our lives.

Ho'oponopono:

This is a Hawaiian healing practice that involves repeating specific phrases or mantras as a way to release negative energy and promote healing.

The phrases often used are *"I love you," "I'm sorry," "Please forgive me," and "Thank you."*

Qigong:

This is a Chinese healing practice that involves the use of movement, breath control, and meditation to balance and cultivate the body's **Chi** (or energy) in order to promote healing and well-being.

NLP (Neuro-Linguistic Programming):

This is a therapeutic technique that uses language, communication, and psychology to help individuals change their thoughts, beliefs, and behaviors in order to achieve specific goals or improve their mental and emotional well-being.

EFT Tapping:

The Emotional Freedom Technique (EFT) is a psychological acupressure technique that involves tapping on specific points on the body in order to release blocked energy and promote healing.

Reiki:

This is a healing practice that involves the use of a practitioner's hands to channel energy into a patient's body in order to promote healing and balance.

Kundalini:

This yoga-based healing practice involves the awakening and rising of the kundalini energy, which is said to reside at the base of the spine.

It's believed that this awakening can bring about spiritual enlightenment and physical healing.

Mudras:

These are hand gestures or positions that are used in yoga and meditation to balance energy and promote healing.

Practitioners believe that human hands are strong electrical connectors and so when connected in a certain way, could control the energies within the body.

Self-Hypnosis:

This is a technique in which an individual is guided into a state of deep relaxation in order to access the subconscious mind and make positive changes to thoughts, behaviors, and emotions.

Auto Suggestion:

This is a technique in which an individual uses positive affirmations to change negative thoughts, beliefs, and behaviors.

Polarity Balancing:

This is a healing practice that involves the use of touch and energy manipulation to balance the body's energy and promote healing.

Touch Therapy:

This is a form of therapy that uses touch to promote relaxation, reduce stress, and improve overall well-being.

Tibetan Singing Bowls:

This is a healing practice that involves the use of singing bowls, which are struck or played with mallets in order to produce a soothing and healing sound.

Music Therapy:

This form of therapy uses music to promote healing and well-being.

Crystal Healing:

This is a healing practice that involves the use of crystals and gemstones to balance and align the body's energy in order to promote healing.

Color Healing:

This is a healing practice that involves the use of color, often in the form of light therapy, to promote healing and balance.

Feng Shui:

This is a Chinese traditional practice that seeks to balance and harmonize the energies in space in correlation with Qigong.

———— ———— ————

Let me boil everything down to its simplest, most concentrated, and easiest-to-digest format for you.

According to **Aura & Pranic Healing, Polarity Balancing, and Reiki,** you have an energy field that can be altered.

Quantum healing, Somatic experience, EFT tapping, and Touch therapy experts believe in similarity, and that there is a connection between mind and body.

Qigong, Feng Shui, Kundalini, and Mudras suggest broadly that meditating and focusing on the mind's stillness could help us take control of our health in multiple dimensions.

The Law of Attraction, Ho'oponopono, Auto Suggestions, Self-Hypnosis, and NLP techniques state from a broader perspective that what you say and think, controls your actions, which in turn create situations that manifest your future.

Tibetan singing bowls and Music therapy show that music or a specific frequency vibration can affect health.

Color and Crystal healing indicates that a certain wavelength of light from a crystal or object could help improve a person's state of mind.

After reading the summary of these techniques, you must have realized what I am trying to communicate to you through this book. –

"You have all the power within you to get whatever you want in your life."
-Omkara Cheetrala
Indian Author and Speaker

I personally have collected some scientific explanations to support and assist these techniques, which were covered in an earlier chapter under the chapter heading **"Myths Debunked."** If you're a sceptic like me and want a logical explanation for everything, re-read that section. Before we go any further into this book, let me share some of my personal coaching experience stories and the benefits of the techniques I mentioned above.

Ho'oponopono:

A Hawaiian healing practice that involves repeating specific phrases or mantras as a way to release negative energy and promote healing.

This is very similar to the Law of Attraction; however, here, more than affirmations, we use phrases often like "I love you," "I'm sorry," "Please forgive me," and "Thank you."

I had a student who is learning **"The Zeroth Apple"** concept from me to manifest her YOUniverse. She became a master of all these concepts, but sadly, she couldn't make her way through them and manifest her desires. She always felt like she was trapped, and nothing worked for her.

No amount of mentoring helped her get out of that loop, so one day I decided to stop mentoring her and just listen to her. I asked her, "Why don't you tell me about your childhood?" She was initially reluctant and asked me how this would help her in her learning and journey towards becoming a Manifestation Master.

I replied, "I am going to teach you how to coach someone and the right questions to ask." She is a great student; she always surrenders to her masters, so she did respond to me.

After three days of continuously asking her about different prominent areas of her life, it strikes me that she is blocking all her energy with something called grief and guilt. She recently lost her mother due to respiratory problems caused by the consumption of sweets, which she presumably gave to her mother.

She is filled with guilt that she killed her mother by feeding her sweets even when the other family members were asking her not to, just because she loves her mother so much.

The same evening, her mother got into severe breathing problems, and she left all of us in the ambulance itself, looking at my student and holding her hands, I asked her, "Do you love your mom?" and she immediately replied, "I wish I hadn't given her those sweets that day."

You see, she is not even ready to admit that she loves her mother to her core; her guilt is literally masking her love. After a session of coaching, I asked her to sit down, handed her a box of tissues, and left the room for her, looking at her, shutting my eyes, nodding my head slowly, and communicating, "It's ok to cry."

She is a very strong lady, never expressing her emotions, and especially the sad ones are even tougher for her, so I gave her space. After around 30 minutes or so, I went back in to see her writing on a piece of paper, "I am sorry; I Love You; Please Forgive and Thank You." I saw a dedicated student up until that day, but only that day did I see a sculpture, forging those phrases on her heart for all time, clearing so much fog from her heart, which condensed into water and overflowed through her eyes.

As I said, she is a very strong lady; she didn't use a single tissue and never cried, as you might think. You are half right. She cried, not because she wanted to, but because she couldn't control herself anymore while writing these lines.

There has been no turning back since. It's a magical thing that she now treats everything that comes her way as a blessing from her mother. She embraces them so tightly and loves all the blessings. By the way, blessings are not always the good times; even the tough times that teach you a lesson for life are blessings.

Please understand that I am limited in explaining everything we discussed during our coaching sessions in one book, but Ho'oponopono is a practice that assists you in unblocking hidden guilt and unknown grief and accepting yourself as you are, allowing the YOUniverse to manifest your desires using **"The Zeroth Apple"** concept.

Self-Hypnosis:

Technique in which an individual is guided into a state of deep relaxation in order to access the subconscious mind and make positive changes to thoughts, behaviors, and emotions.

This is my personal favorite and has been there for ages, especially in Hindu culture. This is exactly what we do in those holy temples—not all temples, but only those built by our ancient forefathers with a pond on the premises (a must).

It was proven that water is one of the most potent energy absorbers when it comes to solar light. It was also discovered recently that water can become slightly poisonous if it takes more than seven bends on its journey. It isn't poisonous enough to kill anyone, but it does cause enough disruption in the human mind and gut.

Bringing these two together is the concept of ponds within the temples. A pond is filled with river water and is stored in stillness under sunlight throughout the day with a cover on it and no continuous flow inside, in which devotees are asked to take baths before worshipping their deities. Even if a temple doesn't have a pond, it may have a river next to the temple with a continuous flow but not with bends, maybe with curves but no bends.

The procedure begins with dipping ourselves in water and then taking rounds iterating the desire you wish to come true, after which you enter a place of silence and fragrance that is almost close to dark to see an idol made of stone that mesmerizes its viewers by the shine and glory, while all of this is happening, there would be some high vibrational sounds, chants being played that you couldn't resist hearing, on top of which you hear a bang bell sound, and...

If you re-read the above paragraph now, imagining that you are reading about a mass hypnosis asylum, it still holds good; give it a try.

Self-hypnosis is just a scaled-down version of this. Out of my research, I know the essence of every single element in that before-mentioned paragraph, which I would explain in my next book, **"The Tharkam,"** if I ever published it. But for this book, let's stick to only the Self-Hypnosis part.

What you must do is identify your desire, define it clearly, and provide details. Record your affirmations, describe how you would like to see your future selves or explain how you are going to perform the next day for your presentation.

Add some binaural beats to the recording so both of them are audible, but your audio dominates the music a little too much.

Listen to this mixed audio created by you every night before sleep, and if you are comfortable sleeping with your earphones on, you could do that too.

What you're doing here is defining your desired **YOUniverse**, attempting to paint a picture of it, hypnotizing yourself to visualize it, and that is self-hypnosis in action for you, saving you hundreds of dollars in research and application fees.

Auto Suggestion:

Technique in which an individual uses positive affirmations to change negative thoughts, beliefs, and behaviors.

I have a client who has the very dignified quality of always being on time. He always told me this: "If I am not on time, I am already late." Assume this person married a woman who barely keeps up with her responsibilities. He gets angry, thinking that she does not respect him or love him because she comes late to a date. He can't make the most of that night's dinner date and also drives back home filling anger within.

He is causing internal turmoil because he adores her so much. I understood the conflict; it is very simple: He loves her for a reason and now gets hurt for the same reason.

These are the value systems he inherited from his mother. Here, if we directly jump into autosuggestion, it requires you to create some affirmations to repeat daily as a habit and visualize the same.

In this case, if I asked him to write down some affirmations in favor of his wife's behavior, I would be performing a great sin as a mentor to him. We need to understand the root cause and try to rip the roots off or provide a different pathway to keep them safe while still redirecting them nicely.

If we try to build affirmations on things we don't approve of, our value systems won't support them, and our beliefs conflict with them, then we are trying to seal a volcano with wax, and we never know when it will open up and expel everything it has built over the course of time.

In this situation, he does not have a bad habit or detrimental pattern, so I must choose the latter approach. As part of our coaching session, I asked him to write down the top 10 qualities that he loves about her partner.

He wrote, "Her Spontaneity," "Her Alertness and Decisiveness," "Her Smart Thinking and Quick Decision-Making skill," and some 7 others.

These are scattered everywhere in his list, which I highlighted with a highlighter and told him this: "See, dear, you love her for some characters that come only when she is late." "If she is always on time, why would she ever be required to be spontaneous? How will she learn quick decision-making skills? When are you going to be alert?"

"Try to not look at her with the lenses you already have if you still want her to be the same: spontaneous, alert, smart, and quick to make decisions."

This makes the autosuggestion simpler and easier for him. From his own will and desire, he must now form some affirmations that reinforce what he likes about her. He formed 10 affirmations, like:

1. I love my wife for her spontaneity.

2. I love my wife's decisiveness.

3. I love when she tries to be herself and is not influenced by someone else's opinion.

And the list goes on. The best part is that we not only helped him avoid failing his relationship, but we also assisted him in determining the best way to use autosuggestion in his life.

We all have this tendency: we fall in love with someone because of their unique characteristics, and once we get close to them, we often tend to clone them into who we are, despite the fact that we were drawn to them in the first place because they are different from us.

This happens more with women, and that concerns me a lot. Many girls come to me after a broken relationship, and when I ask them, "What made you attracted to him?" She said, "He is very nice and smart; he talks first and makes me feel comfortable even before he knows who I am." "He helps everyone and fights for his friends." "He made me feel like me when he was around."

Well, why did you break up with him? "Because he is being the same with other women and he is still getting into fights for his friends without thinking about me, what will happen to me if something happens to him in a fight?"

Of course, he will; that is what he is. If you do not want him to be so with other girls, you should find someone who will do all of these things as well as some particularly important things only with you.

Especially for men, sharing where he wants to go. What is his dream place? What is his next big goal? Is tough. Men usually don't discuss these topics with women, but if he does, you might have a chance. But yet, please check if he is doing that with every other woman before getting into the relationship, if so better find someone else.

But once you get into it, don't try to break it up or suppress your emotions; instead, use autosuggestion to manifest a beautiful, bonded **YOUniverse** into your life with the new knowledge you learned from **"The Zeroth Apple"** concept.

If in case you are looking for the correct technique and some hand-held support from me, you can reach me at OmkaraCheerala.com or Google Omkara Cheetrala.

Please subscribe to my Author Page on Amazon or follow me on Social Media, so you shall be informed about the coming parts of this 7 books series inside which I will be revealing the secrets of **'The Zeroth Apple'** exclusively for each area of life in detail.

Summary:

❖ According to **Aura & Pranic Healing, Polarity Balancing, and Reiki,** you have an energy field that can be altered.

❖ **Quantum healing, Somatic experience, EFT tapping, and Touch therapy** experts believe in similarity, that there is a connection between mind and body.

❖ **Qigong, Feng Shui, Kundalini, and Mudras** suggest broadly that meditating and focusing on the mind's stillness could help us take control of our health in multiple dimensions.

❖ **The Law of Attraction, Ho'oponopono, Auto Suggestions, Self-Hypnosis, and NLP** techniques state from a broader perspective that what you say and think controls your actions, which in turn create situations that manifest your future.

❖ **Tibetan singing bowls and music therapy** show that music or a specific frequency vibration can affect health.

❖ **Color and crystal healing** indicate that a certain wavelength of light from a crystal or object could help improve a person's state of mind.

PART THREE: HOW AND HOW NOT TO?

CHAPTER 6:
RULES OF THE YOUNIVERSE

Just like any other universe, the **YOUniverse** also has some rules. These rules are simple, straightforward, and easy to understand, yet fundamental.

There are 3 rules that can make your **YOUniverse** flourish if you follow them, or they can break your **YOUniverse** if you try to bend them.

Keep this in mind: Rules aren't made to be broken! It may sound cool to say, "Rules are made to break," but practically, rules are made to guide life, harmony, and peace. So, please, never ever try to get around these rules, period.

Rule 1: Your YOUniverse must obey the 12 Laws of the Universe

Now you must be wondering what these Laws of the Universe are. Before we get into them, understand this: These are the "laws," not the rules; as I said earlier, you may bend the rules, which I won't recommend, but you can in some instances; as for the laws, sorry, nothing beyond the laws can happen.

It is something like "*The Law of Gravity.*" Whether you believe it or not, it doesn't matter; once you climb up to the 5th floor and jump out of the window and scream your lungs out, "I don't believe you, Gravity," it will pull you down.

Now that we have aviation marvels that we see in our daily commute, aren't they denying "*The Law of Gravity*"?

No, it isn't.

They are playing along with nature; they are exerting enough upward force, precisely equal to the weight on board compared to the gravitational pull accounted for by the buoyancy force of the air and dozens of other parameters.

In simple terms, there is no, I repeat, "no" aviation structure that was ever built that could defy "the law of gravity" and would never be built. I am confident that you now have a better understanding of the rules and laws.

So, here are the 12 Laws of the Universe that should be maintained and always followed while you create your **YOUniverse:**

The Law of Oneness: This law states that everything in the universe is connected and that we are all part of one unified whole.

The Law of Vibration: This law states that everything in the universe vibrates at a specific frequency and that our thoughts and feelings can affect the vibration we emit.

The Law of Action: This law states that we must act to manifest our desires and that inaction will prevent us from achieving our goals.

The Law of Correspondence: This law states that our outer world reflects our inner world and that we can change our circumstances by changing our thoughts and beliefs.

The Law of Cause and Effect: This law states that every action has a corresponding reaction and that we are responsible for the consequences of our actions.

The Law of Compensation: This law states that we will receive back in kind what we put out into the world, whether it be positive or negative.

It also states that the universe has a way of balancing out or compensating for the actions and efforts of individuals.

This law is often associated with the idea that people will be rewarded for their good deeds and hard work and will face consequences for their negative actions.

The Law of Attraction: This law states that we attract into our lives whatever we focus on, whether it be positive or negative.

The Law of Perpetual Transmutation of Energy: This law states that energy is constantly changing and transforming and that we have the power to direct this energy in a positive or negative direction.

The Law of Relativity: This law states that everything is relative to something else. Everything is neutral in nature; we give meaning to them "Good" or "Bad" relative to what we perceive or feel.

The Law of Gender/ Giving and Receiving: This law states that everything in the universe has both masculine and feminine qualities and that these qualities must be balanced to manifest our desires.

Similar to Masculine and Feminine, Giving and Receiving is also the pair of opposite energies that prevails in association with each other and cannot exist alone.

The Law of Polarity/ Yin and Yang: This law states that everything in the universe has an opposite and that these opposites are interconnected and dependent on each other.

The Law of Rhythm/ Perpetual Motion: This law states that everything in the universe moves in cycles and that these cycles influence the manifestation of our desires.

This law also states that nothing could move or be in motion forever without external influence at periodic intervals of time.

"By using the Law of Attraction, you can create the life you desire and achieve your goals and dreams."
-Dr. Joseph Murphy (1898-1981)
Irish American Author and New Thought Minister

Rule 2: Follow "The Rule of Value Equilibrium"

Let's say I have a kg of cotton and a kg of iron. Which one weighs more? If you said iron, please read it again.

Both weigh the same, however, but if I asked you to pay me the same amount for cotton that you are paying for iron, would you accept that transaction? Or even a transaction the other way around—would you even accept that?

Why not? Because, as you are aware, the value of iron is significantly higher than that of cotton.

If I tell you that cotton is the rarest of all materials and you are a typical cotton collector (I'm not sure if there is such a hobby, but for the sake of argument, it's best to go with the flow), you may now pay me more than I could ever imagine.

The message I want to put forth is very simple: if you want to receive a certain value from your YOUniverse, give it up front. Let that sink in; it is a literal exchange, just like when you only got a half-bottle of water on a sunny mid-day in the desert when you came across a bore pump with cardboard saying, "Give all that you have and get more than what you need."

Give all that you have and get more than what you need.
-Omkara Cheetrala
Indian Author and Speaker

Now you have two choices: either get all in and put that half-full bottle of water into the bore pump and start plunging the handle or move ahead with that half-filled water bottle.

If you move ahead without going all in, what are the odds? You may find some more sand, but not water. If I were in that situation, I would give everything I had, not because I trust the man who put up the board, but to ensure that if it's a forgery, I will at least help the next passerby by changing the note to, "You are doing great; please move on; this pump didn't work when I tried."

The man in this story did exactly what I did: he went all in, poured in all the water he could get his hands on, and began cranking the handle; nothing came out, but he never stopped. The moment he felt like giving up, the pump started gushing out water like a fountain.

He filled his bottle after he cleared his thrust and continued his journey, but just before that, he did this.

He wrote a note on top of the one that's already there, and it goes like this: "You can trust this man."

Now, please don't ask, like my coaching prodigies, "Where did the markers come from?" It is a story, a story to let you understand the Law of Value Equilibrium.

Giving all that you have before you seek more than what you want is the real way to make your **YOUniverse** work.

Also, understand that the value is perceived by the seeker; just as Cotton's value varied between a regular vendor and a collector, the value of what you give varies based on the receiver.

What do I mean by that? The value you are adding to the **YOUniverse** by donating $1,000 or some INR 50,000 to an orphanage's administrator, who runs the place as a job, is much diminished when compared to the $1 or some INR 50 you gave away to a person in the hospital purchasing medicine who is short of INR 50.

I am not saying that donating to a home is bad; all that I am trying to tell you here is that the seeker changes the value of what you are giving.

Let me make it even simpler for you: If you are expecting love from someone, love someone unconditionally. If you are looking forward to an appreciation from your manager or client, appreciate that chef at the diner restaurant, your team member, or that valet parking guy.

If you are looking for money in your life, give it to a seeker. A seeker is not always a homeless person; a friend of yours whose father is in the hospital is a seeker; a father buying a doll for his daughter who is short of money can add many times more value to your donation than the organization that runs the temple, church, or mosque.

In simple terms, "The Law of Value Equilibrium" has to say just this: "Give me what you want before you get more than what you need," and that is an abundant life, my friend.

"Your thoughts and feelings are powerful magnets that attract to you the people, circumstances, and events that are in harmony with them."
-Dr. Joseph Murphy (1898-1981)
Irish American Author and New Thought Minister

Rule 3: Do not waste your time trying to create something that is beyond your Circle of Influence

I understand and believe what I'm saying because I've been there myself, attempting to influence some issues that concern me.

Let's say a roommate of mine is continuously trying to drain my energy with his negative thoughts, energy, frequency, and discussions. It indeed concerns me, no doubt about it, but the problem began when I tried to create a better positive and enriching world for him.

I tried to inform him about the seminar; I injected literally forcefully some intellectually positive comments into our discussions; he was unable to withstand my constant push and is now unhappy because he feels like he is living someone else's life by trying to be positive and speaking of enriching ideas.

What could I do? Shall I still push him harder and harder? Or leave him there and let him come back when he wants to come back; till then, isolate me from such conversations or even change my room at some point in time.

When I coached people with my techniques and told them this story, they started telling me, "Omkara!" "You must have stayed with him and pushed him a little further." If I had done that, he would have never come back to me as a different person seeking growth and positivity.

As a coach or a teacher, my responsibility is not to teach someone something; it is to clear their thoughts, let them stay still, and give them the fragrance, taste, and sound of what goodness is like! Once they feel it, they will find it.

I coached a lot of drunkards; I never told them that drinking is bad. I showed them how they could enjoy themselves without alcohol and still be social.

But after a session ended, a student of mine came to me and asked me, "Omkara!" "What if the person you live with is your parent and you can't avoid them, yet you can't get into their drama and negativity?"

That night was a sleepless night for me. Not because I failed to answer him, but because somewhere down in my heart, I too feel the same. I spoke to a couple of friends, and they too feel the same. Every middle-class child aspiring to grow feels alike because middle-class parents are programmed to enjoy what they have with minimal to almost no risk appetite. When aspiring kids want to grow in that environment, it is obvious for them to feel likewise.

Next week, when the student came back to me for his session, I gave him a glass of water added in it, ashes and too much salt and asked him to fill that glass with clean, drinkable water. But the catch is, yes, there is a catch; there is always a catch. The catch is that you can't turn the glass upside down or leave the glass, and that's all.

He tried all possible alternatives that are possibly running through your head right now. After an hour and nearly 20 failed attempts, I called him and told him something, and in a moment, he figured it out.

Focus on what you want but not what you have
-Omkara Cheetrala
Indian Author and Speaker

Focus on what you need, not on what you got:

Friends, focus on what you need, not what you have! You may have a lot of dirt on your plate right now, but if you keep focusing on it, you are vibrating at a dirty frequency, and you end up attracting dirt.

If you want cleanliness, focus on cleanliness, and your dirt will be washed away.

If you want clear water, focus on clear water, not the muddy water that you have.

He rushed into my kitchen and started holding the glass under the running tap. The glass started to overflow, vomiting every new freshwater drop that was coming its way, but the freshwater coming in was too much, and by the time the ashy, salty water vomited one drop of fresh water, a flow of fresh water started to flow down.

The freshwater began to flow down, churning the ashy, salty water in and out and pushing out a lot of water, both good and bad.

After maybe 10 minutes, the bottom of the glass started to appear. After another 5 minutes, the glass looks like it has lost half of its ashes and salt. He waited long enough, and now he has a glass full of fresh water to drink.

After that, I told him, "Today's coaching is done; now you can go home; but understand this: just because the glass has undrinkable water, you don't have to leave it all the time and move on; if you have the patience that it takes and if you wish to wait for longer, you can get fresh water into your parent's life as well."

The fulfilment I felt in my heart that day cannot be bought with all the wealth on this planet.

Well, if someone contains the power to influence someone's **YOUniverse**, what is this rule all about? If you read my rule, it states: "Don't waste your time trying to create something that is beyond your Circle of Influence."

Serving no food is sometimes better than serving half-baked:

You can surely impact someone's **YOUniverse**, but the catch is, do you have the patience that it takes? Do you have mastery over your **YOUniverse**? Without being played by their **YOUniverse**, could you influence them?

Baba Totapuri did the same, as a regional story among hundreds of other narrations goes this way: On a bright day, just like every other day, Baba Totapuri has been meditating all day but seems to be expecting someone to meet him that day. After noon, there was a young man standing in front of Baba without speaking a word. A young man who has been in search of truth and a real purpose for wisdom

He was told that there is a Baba who could help him answer all his questions, and so he came here today to find out if that Baba is true and honest in the first place.

But to his surprise, the Baba never opened his eyes but said something along similar lines to this: "Oh! So, it took you this long to come? Well! Anyway, you finally arrived at the right place; I have been waiting for you for a long time now." You could read the rest of the story in the biography of Swami Vivekananda's teacher, Ramakrishna Paramahamsa. The young boy was Ramakrishna Paramahamsa.

Baba Totapuri, who was acclaimed to be wiser, smarter, and more intricately connected to the Divine, must wait a long time to make a dent in Ramakrishna's **YOUniverse** and reach him. Then the question arises: how much patience do you have to impact someone else's **YOUniverse?**

Some relationships, especially those based on unconditional love, such as those between parents, siblings, friends, and spouses, cannot be severed.

Parents never gave birth to us only because they thought we could be successful; they never raised us to give them back the investment they had into us.

Siblings never played with us because we gave them a treat, or they could get something back.

They do that unconditionally. Except in rare circumstances, I've never seen a sibling curse a brother or sister; they can't because they've been in unconditional love for many years.

The same applies to childhood friends and spouses; they would never ever even dream of harming you; they do love you, in the majority of cases, it may not be unconditional.

For them, you could and should be patient and try to impact and influence their **YOUniverse**. It should not, however, collapse your **YOUniverse**. To make it simple and clear, let me tell you the simplest way to do the right thing, but yes, sometimes the right things aren't easy things.

If you wish to influence someone's YOUniverse:

If you want to influence someone's **YOUniverse** because they stay with you the majority of the time in a day, stay with them and don't push them to know this secret **YOUniverse** concept; they will rather run far away from this just like those ashes and salty water tried to repel clean water.

But you could certainly do what my student did with consistency, but by consistency, I didn't mean pushing them beyond their will; I meant subconsciously imprinting on them the value, results, and outcomes of this secret world.

Create curiosity and assist them in developing that interest in themselves without their knowledge. Hold this book in your hand at all times and walk around them; bring it to the dinner table; please don't read it; and never try to forcefully inject something without their permission; just bring it to the dinner table.

Set the book's cover image as your lock screen or home screen. Maybe take a print of it and place it in the hall under the TV remote. Take multiple copies of the cover and place them below the mirror on the dressing table.

And, after describing the cover to them, ask them if they found it that you intentionally kept out of their reach.

What you are doing here is just an act of building curiosity and letting them ask you just one question: "What is that book?"

Don't answer them; tell them they may not understand it even if you explain this in your mother tongue because to understand this, you must be open and ready to digest. Be polite, don't hurt their ego, and just tell them the truth that this isn't a topic for chatting but a concept for life that needs dedicated focus.

They won't be curious anymore; repeat this after a break. Tell them I restarted reading this concept and was unable to find it; did you find it?

The curiosity builds, and there will be a day when you will be asked, "I am sitting here right now, open and ready. Tell me what's great in that book."

If they can read for themselves, hand them this copy and ask them to read it; if not, you can read the summary pages for them if they can't read for themselves.

Never speak about this book in public

By the way, do not speak about this concept at all to anyone in your circle until you have finished reading it yourself from start to finish. I can explain to you why. I used to be that kid who wanted to read as many books as possible, but when I knew the context and snippets of the book, I would never read it; I would buy the book but not thoroughly read it.

So, when I wanted to read a book, I used to ask my friends for recommendations, which I would buy but never read because they recommended it alongside some critical context that would most likely be the crux. I will never have the same enthusiasm to read this book from beginning to end once I know the twist.

Even if I did read, having never read the entirety of the book, I began applying those concepts solely based on my friend's words and how he described them. English is a very tricky language, my friend; if you read the same sentence when in a good mood, it would sound a certain way, and when the same message was sent by someone you have a predefined image of, it would sound very different.

It is because we associate value with the words we read or hear. My friend may have read the book in a particular mood, envisioning the author as a specific person to assist with specific problems, and then explains it to me in the same tone and thought process. That may not be the problem for which I am looking for a solution; that may not be the actual image of that author; that may not be the entire essence of the book; and there may be a lot hidden in it.

Since knowing this, I stopped asking anyone for suggestions. Instead, I go through Google and find their interviews, talks, websites, etc., to get a feel for who they are and what they have to offer, and then select a book.

So, see, my friend, even if you read this book thoroughly, it is always better to ask them to read the book on their own without expecting anything. You may have picked this book to create a financially rich **YOUniverse**; he may need it to create a healthy **YOUniverse**; or maybe his need is to create a relationship rich **YOUniverse**. We never know.

All we know is that they seem to be in need of this book's help, which I am providing to them. In fact, my publisher must be very unhappy by now, looking at the above paragraph, because I wasn't promoting you to buy a new book but to hand them your copy. Because, my friend, I am not here to sell books and make money; I am here to make an impact on your life, which in turn can change the lives of a generation and an upcoming family from you.

Summary:

- ❖ Just like any other universe, your YOUniverse also has 3 rules.

- ❖ **Rule 1:** Your YOUniverse must obey the 12 Laws of the Universe.

- ❖ **Rule 2:** Follow "The Rule of Equilibrium": It is not how much quantity you give; it is how much quality value you provide into the YOUniverse that matters and comes back to you at the right time.

- ❖ **Rule 3:** Don't waste your time trying to create something that is beyond your Circle of Influence, unless they are your unconditionally loving blessings.

- ❖ Focus on what you need, not what you have. If you have no money, never focus on the lack of money; focus on the abundance of money.

- ❖ If you wish to influence someone's YOUniverse, don't try to inject the concept of this book into them but rather try to propel them with curiosity and enthusiasm.

- ❖ Never speak about this book in public until you finish reading it thoroughly from start to finish.

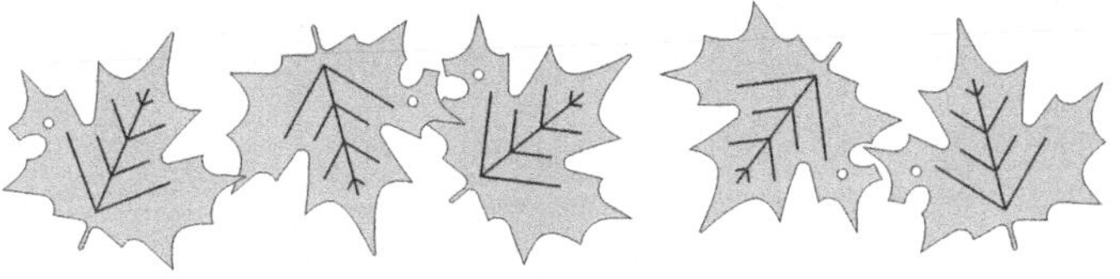

CHAPTER 7:
HOW TO CREATE YOUR YOUNIVERSE.

Pareto Pattern

It was the year 1896, and Vilfredo Pareto, an Italian, was busy harvesting peas in his garden when he made an interesting observation. He noticed that some peapods had a lot more peas in them than others.

On counting the number of peas in each peapod, he found that 80% of the peas came from only 20% of the peapods. Now, if there are 10 peapods with 50 peas in total, we would expect that each peapod would have 5 peas in it.

In other words, we would expect that each peapod would (more or less) have the same number of peas in it. But Vilfredo found that 20% of the peapods (i.e., 2 out of the 10 peapods) had 80% of the peas (40 out of the 50 peas).

Vilfredo was an economist, and he noticed the same pattern in how wealth was distributed in Italy. He found that 20% of the people in Italy owned 80% of the land. These 20% were very wealthy! The remaining 80% of the population owned only 20% of the land.

This pattern still holds true today. In most economies, a small group of people own most of the wealth.

This 80/20 principle is now known as the "Pareto Principle." It simply states that "20% of the efforts will give you 80% of the results.".

"The universe is full of magical things patiently waiting for our wits to grow sharper."
- Eden Phillpotts (1862-1960)
English Author, Poet, and Playwright

Golden Ratio Pattern

Euclid was obsessed with understanding the mysteries of the universe and spent most of his time studying mathematics and geometry. One day, as he was studying the petals of a flower, the answer finally came to him. The proportion he had been looking for was the **GOLDEN RATIO**, a unique number that's about 1.618. It's a number that we can see all around us in nature and art.

When we divide a line into two parts, the ratio of the longer part to the smaller part is the same as the ratio of the whole line to the longer part.

This ratio is found in things like the way leaves grow on a plant, the shape of seashells, and even in the human body.

It's a really cool number that helps us understand the patterns and beauty in the world around us! The discovery of the Golden Ratio was a turning point in both the history of math and the history of humanity. It will always be remembered as a testament to the power of human curiosity, determination, and imagination.

"All the patterns of nature repeat themselves everywhere and on every scale."
- Edward Tufte (1912-1999)
American statistician and professor emeritus of political science, statistics, and computer science at Yale University

---

Chaos Pattern

In the 1960s, a young mathematician named Edward Lorenz was working on computer models of weather patterns at MIT. He had been running simulations for months to try to figure out why the atmosphere seems to act in such a complicated and random way.

One day, as he was analyzing the results of one of his simulations, he noticed something strange. He had run the exact same set of initial conditions twice, but the two simulations produced entirely different outcomes. Puzzled, he reran the simulation, this time with the initial conditions rounded off to three decimal places instead of six. To his surprise, the results matched the first simulation exactly.

This realization hit him like a bolt of lightning. He understood that trivial differences in initial conditions could lead to vastly different outcomes in complex systems, a concept later known as **The Butterfly Effect**. This discovery led him to develop the concept of **Chaos Theory**, which would go on to have a profound impact on fields as varied as weather forecasting, economics, and physics.

"The universe is built on a plan the profound symmetry of which is somehow present in the inner structure of our intellect."
- Paul Valery (aka: Ambroise-Paul-Toussaint-Jules Valéry) (1871-1945)
Major Figure of French Poetry

Fractals' Pattern

It was the early 1970s, and a young mathematician named Benoit Mandelbrot was working at IBM's research lab in New York. He had always been interested in patterns in nature, like how the branches of a tree or the shape of a coastline had the same shape over and over again.

One day, while studying images generated by a computer program, he noticed a strange repeating pattern. Intrigued, he dove deeper into his research and discovered **The Concept of Fractals**. He found that these fractals, unlike the geometric shapes he had studied before, were rough and irregular, yet they still possessed a self-similarity across scales.

Fractals are repeating patterns that get smaller and smaller each time they repeat themselves, and they can be found all around us in nature and used in many different ways.

"In nature, nothing is perfect, and everything is perfect. Trees can be contorted, bent in weird ways, and they're still beautiful."
- Alice Walker (1900-1982)
American Author, Poet, and Social Activist.

Yin-Yang Pattern

Long ago in ancient China, there was a wise and learned scholar named Ming. He had devoted his life to the study of philosophy and the mysteries of the universe. Despite his wealth of knowledge, Ming felt unfulfilled, as though there was a missing piece to the puzzle of existence that he had yet to uncover.

One day, while on a walk in the countryside, Ming came across a small pond. As he sat down to rest beside it, he noticed the reflection of the sky above. And as he sat there in contemplative silence, the sun and clouds began to shift, revealing a perfect balance of light and dark, movement and stillness.

Ming was struck by this scene of **Yin and Yang** in perfect harmony and realized that this balance was the missing piece he had been searching for. He immediately returned to his studies and began researching this concept, which he called the **"Yin-Yang"**, determined to uncover its secrets, and share his discovery with others.

As Ming dove deeper into his research, he encountered much resistance from other scholars and even his own family, who believed his ideas were heretical. But Ming refused to be discouraged and continued to delve deeper, even as his own health began to deteriorate.

It was during a particularly dark time, as he lay on his deathbed, that Ming finally understood the true meaning of the Yin-Yang. He saw that life and death, joy, and sorrow, were all part of the same balance, and that true wisdom came from embracing the entirety of existence.

Ming passed away peacefully, knowing that his discovery would live on and bring balance and understanding to countless generations to come. His ideas about the Yin-Yang would shape Chinese philosophy and culture for hundreds of years, and he would be remembered as a genius who figured out how the universe worked.

The story of Ming and his discovery of Yin and Yang is an important chapter in Chinese history and a representation of the Chinese cosmological view of the balance of the universe. The story takes a dramatic turn, with added drama and emotions to make it more interesting, but the basic idea of the discovery of the Yin Yang concept and its impact is genuine.

"Nature is an endless combination and repetition of a very few laws."
- Ralph Waldo Emerson (1803-1888)
American Philosopher, Lecturer, and Poet

Importance of Patterns in YOUniverse

By now you must be thinking, "Why am I reading so many stories related to different patterns?" But still, if you are reading this after completing the above stories, then, well, you must have understood at least one of the lessons below, if not all:

1. This whole universe is filled with patterns.

2. Nature has answers to all the questions we have.

3. Patterns are not just interesting; they are groundbreaking.

How Patterns affect your YOUniverse

Let's now investigate 'How this new knowledge of yours could help you create your **YOUniverse?**'

To create your **YOUniverse** alongside the rules you studied in the previous chapters, you must follow these simple steps:

Step 1: Define your YOUniverse.

Defining the **YOUniverse** may sound simple and straightforward, but the key is in the details. Define your desired **YOUniverse** with as many details as possible for your imaginative brain.

When looking for a house, be specific about how many square yards you require. How many floors? How many rooms?

When you plan to manifest a specific amount of money into your **YOUniverse**, be specific about the amount, and many people do this until now and then forget to follow the next important step, which is to assign emotion and value to every penny.

Why do you require INR 50,000 (approximately $1,000)? If that's what you want to manifest in your **YOUniverse**, divide it clearly into your expenses, mortgage, health, and travel plan. Only after you have properly budgeted that amount should you consider this step completed.

Kindly do not ask for more money, more time, or more peace of mind. Be specific. For someone, 50 grand would be less, and for someone else, it could be a life-changing extra 50 grand. Without you being specific, how shall that be manifested in your **YOUniverse**? Not only **YOUniverse**, but you also would wonder yourself, 'What did I mean when I meant more money?' if you look at that desire after a 6-month period.

No amount of magic is going to bring a bag of cash and drop it in front of your door; it is you who is going to bring that money into your life, so it is imperative to give yourself the right instructions, clear directions, and proper guidelines to reach the goal.

It is as simple as looking at Google Maps for a moment and driving into a village full of streets. You can of course remember the next turn and the next 10 turns, but for sure, 2 out of every 5 times, you would end up at the next or opposite building, or even behind the building you should actually reach. Do you want that to happen to you when it comes to your desire?

If you are fine with that, then you need to rethink what you call "desire." It is just a wish, not a desire. We can only manifest desires into our **YOUniverses**, not simple hopes or wishes. If you are looking for magic that will grant you all of your wishes at once, this book is not for you...

Step 2: Write it down.

Well, it may sound old-fashioned but there is a lot of science hidden in it.

You can imagine an incomplete circle, but you never draw an incomplete circle.
-Omkara Cheetrala
Indian Author and Speaker

Try to imagine a bicycle with three wheels perpendicular to each other something like the front and back wheels being perpendicular to each other, as well as a wheel on the top of the bicycle that is now perpendicular to both wheels!

Now, try to draw the same thing on a piece of paper. If you have done that, you will start to wonder: is this a bicycle anymore? Can someone ride on this? Is this practically possible?

This is as simple as that. While you imagine, you could imagine possibly a hundred things in your brain; there is no problem with it. But only when you try to put them on paper and start to think, that is when your conscious, logical mind starts questioning you.

I am asking you to do the same with your desire to manifest into your **YOUniverse**. Write it down. I cannot possibly cover all possible combinations where someone could go wrong unless I coach them personally; humanly, it isn't possible either. So, there could be some details you are missing in your Step 1 while writing, and I may not have addressed them all in Step 1 either.

This step will help you get to those missing details. When you thought of more money, now when I ask you to write it down with details, you shall start asking yourself, "How much money?" "What is that money for?" "Where do I spend that money?"

In other words, you would start budgeting the money you are going to manifest; you would start to think like you already have that money; you would plan like you possess that money with you right now, which brings us down to Step 4; but before that, let's look at Step 3.

Step 3: Assign an emotion to your written desire.

Everything you are attempting to manifest in your YOUniverse is because you love it, want it more, and desire it. Then there has to be some positive emotion attached to it, which you already have; I am asking you to identify that.

You felt happy when you wrote "loving partner"; now try to amplify it with specifics. "A loving partner who respects me in public and cares for me in private." Magnify the emotion by intensifying the details. "An emotionally interdependent, loving, caring partner who is 5'10" tall and fairly toned Asian with charming eyes and a manly voice that combines smartness and wisdom."

By adding more details, what you are doing here is intensifying the intertwined emotions within you and making yourself clear on what you want, and without your knowing it, you are also clearly articulating what you don't want too, which is predominantly important while you define your desire.

I have a female client who always speaks about her dream husband. She wanted him to be caring, loving, smart, manly, handsome, muscular, tall, smart, and everything else. I asked her, as a part of my coaching exercise, to write down her description of her dream boyfriend or husband on a piece of paper. The catch is that she has to write it down 100 times.

She successfully did that, but when she came back and I asked her to now describe her dream boyfriend or husband, she described the same without any emotion in her words. She said that at first, it was exciting, but after a point of time, she became numb to that description.

After a session of visualization with me, I asked her once again to write down the dream boyfriend's description 100 times, but this time the catch is that after every 5 times, she adds one more detail to it. At first, she was resistant as she had to add 20 detail points to her description, but as I insisted, she did it.

Instead of becoming numb after the first 25, she became excited; in fact, after every five times she finished writing the description, she began biting her lips, enjoying herself while writing and describing. At the end of my session, she also revealed that she felt like drawing his dream boyfriend.

She would now be looking for such a man and not getting into any risky relationships where she has to give it a try, realize it won't work, and then move on to someone else because her emotion towards that has been amplified many times.

She is now clear about whom she wants and also about whom she doesn't want. Isn't it important? Similarly, the same is true for wealth, a job, health, or anything else.

Let me actually demonstrate the real impact of emotion. "Do you know that people cannot smell through their nose when they try to touch it with their tongue? See, isn't it true? Oh, is it not? Were you able to smell something? There isn't any such study, but look how nice, cute, intspeconly and thezerapply you are." These are the exact lines I said in my "*Toastmasters International Speech Contest*" where I won, of course, first prize, and after 3 minutes of my speech, I revealed something shocking and surprising, which you too are going to experience right now.

There are no words called "intspeconly" or "thezerapply." They are actually the first 3 letters of "International Speech Contest" and "The Zeroth Apple." But isn't it because you're in a certain frame of mind and the lines and words around it give it meaning? That's what we do in our daily lives.

Imagine I am scolding you in a language you don't understand; in fact, I am screaming my lungs out, but what you understand is only my emotion. If you don't even know me or how I express my feelings, you may also think I am mad and that I am trying to communicate with you, or even trying to give you a compliment, or helping someone else behind you with directions, or anything else. You may also laugh at me.

Let's say you get upset because you understand what I meant, but wait a minute, the words are the same, you and I are the same people, the place, environment, surroundings, pronunciation, syllables, facial expressions, hand gestures, tone, volume, and everything else is the same, but your response is completely different. Why? Because you know the meaning of that word and have associated emotion with it.

I used to have a client who was brought up in a conservative family and had some predefined notions about certain words, like manipulation, wealthy, and wine. When I asked him to write something and he came up to me with an elaborated version of the word "manipulation," I realized this and asked him to strike out everything he elaborated and replace it with the word and rewrite the story. Guess what? His story has become all negative right now.

Previously, he wrote something along the lines of, "The protagonist was able to manage and convince the antagonist that he does have the antagonist's child and successfully regained custody of his wife back."

But the rewritten story sounded like this: "The protagonist manipulated the antagonist to win and got his wife back, along with guilt." He was a good man till then, but he is no longer a good man.

It's not surprising to me; I know what to do, and I did it, but at the end of the story, I want to show you how powerful emotions are; they can easily make or break your **YOUniverse**.

I have many clients who are employees who want to do a better job but end up in a toxic bossy organization or team. The simple thing is that they want a better job, but they are never clear about what "better" means to them. Some manifested a good-paying job yet the same bossy manager; some manifested a peaceful environment but at the cost of their health due to shifts in nature and round-the-clock support projects.

Step 4: Talk, Walk, Smell, Think and Behave as if you already possess what you desire.

"The man who can visualize his own future and make it conform to his desires is the one who achieves success."
-William Walker Atkinson (1862-1932)
American Lawyer and New Thought Author

As I was saying at the end of Step 2 when you start to add details, you start to add emotions to them, and at the same time, you start to work as if you already have them.

Let's say you wanted a better job with good pay and a healthy environment where your fullest potential was identified and appreciated at the same time.

Now, before you search for such a job, behave as if you are enjoying that kind of role. You are not only subconsciously imprinting what you want, but also sending a message to the YOUniverse about how well you are prepared to appreciate when you receive what you desired.

Next time when you are talking to someone, stop complaining about your boss and rather speak highly about the positives. I am not asking you to "Fake it until you make it. But just stop complaining about your boss and rather speak highly about the positives.

Let me try something new with you for the first time. Look around and observe the room you are in right now. Set a limit until a point where you can see clearly; once done, scan the whole room and come back to this book.

Now identify seven items that are red in color in this room within the limits you set for yourself. You do not need to record them anywhere; you just need to memorize them, that's all.

Now that you are done with this, I want you to repeat the same motion, but this time with your eyes closed. Instructions are here; I trust you and I hope you do it with me. Now, close your eyes after reading this paragraph. Please do not lift your head now; keeping your head bent down into the book, I want you to identify seven items that are purple in color in the room within the limits you set with your eyes shut.

No cheating, please...

I wish I could be next to you to see how your eyeballs move around while you try to recall the purple items. We have a tendency to assign a location to a color and an emotion.

Lift your head up now and validate your responses with what you thought. How many did you get right? Many would get barely 3, some would get 5, and a few would get all 7 items.

This exercise has two levels of depth. The first one teaches you that "when you are focusing on the red-colored items, your brain never captures any purple-colored items."

Even though you are an amazing observer, if you got all 7 purple-colored items, when you closed your eyes, you would only see the purple-colored items in your visuals but not the previous, red-colored items unless you assigned a reference between them.

This is how your brain works; it finds everything that reinforces what you focus on, which is why you find many Porsches on the road after reading a news article on Porsche cars, and why you see number 7 everywhere because I used it everywhere in my book and forced you to see the same thing.

Now let's use this to our advantage and focus on the better things in your job that you have hated so far. Let the manager be so bossy, but maybe your colleagues are good; let the pay be less; your office is close to the nearest cinema; let the shifts be round the clock; you are now getting a cab, so you don't need to drive.

By always looking at the bright side and being positive and optimistic, you attract people towards you, and you sound like a friendly person to work with. Who would not want to work with a friendly, positive, energetic, smiling person?

I'm not saying that a manager will magically come to you and appreciate your nature, offering you a role in their team; I'm saying that there could be that one friend who loves your energy, has now left the company, learned about an opening that might fit your profile, and so refers you.

But in the first place, to make all this happen, behave as if you are already working in such an environment, or, in other words, as if you already possess what you are desiring for.

Step 5: Identify Patterns and Inject them.

"The patterns of nature, of which man is a part, are never destroyed, but are constantly changing, constantly adapting to new conditions."
- Rachel Carson (1907-1964)
American marine biologist, author, and conservationist.

This is the most important and decisive step in this chapter, which is why you read so many stories earlier in it. Patterns are everywhere—in the universe and inside you and me, too—but they are exhibited as behaviors.

I am not talking about habits; I am referring to patterns. The fundamental difference between a habit and a pattern is that habits are formed by repeatedly performing an action, while patterns are formed by repeating a sequence of actions or events.

A habit is a behavior that has become so automatic that we perform it without thinking about it. Habits can be good or bad, such as brushing your teeth every morning or biting your nails when you're nervous. Habits are usually made and kept through a system of rewards, which makes them more unconscious and automatic.

A pattern, on the other hand, is the regularity or repetition of events or actions. Patterns can be found in many areas, such as nature, art, music, and even our everyday lives. Patterns can be observed and analyzed, but they don't involve the same level of repetition as habits do.

In conclusion, both habits and patterns involve repetition, but habits are made by doing the same thing over and over again and are kept going by rewards, while patterns are made by repeating a sequence of actions or events and can be seen and studied.

In simple terms, balancing a motorcycle while riding is a subconscious action that rewards you for reaching your destination with less effort, whereas honking the horn while applying breaks and releasing the throttle while taking turns is a pattern involving a sequence of actions.

In this step, you will need to identify some of the patterns you noticed while practicing Step 4 and forcefully inject them to amplify the effect and use the power of patterns to your advantage.

For example, when you are trying to "talk, walk, and behave" as if you are already promoted to that role, you will have to speak in a certain way, be with certain people, and talk at a certain level of detail and confidentiality.

All those come with a sequence of actions, and those are all the patterns you need to identify and make a note of. You may have done them twice in the last week, if not in the same sequence, but now that you have identified them, you are going to forcefully inject them into your daily activities.

Something like asking those certain people to come to join you for lunch and discussing carpooling with those certain people while maintaining a certain level of confidentiality about your personal life, maybe.

Now that is a pattern; find more and repeat them again and again. Inject them everywhere possible until they become normal, becoming sub-consciously imprinted.

Step 6: Break the old destructive patterns.

"As you become more aware of your thoughts and how they create your reality, you'll be able to create anything you want."
-Louise L. Hay (1926-2017)
American Self-help Author and Motivational Speaker

Patterns used to your advantage will undoubtedly assist you in manifesting your desired **YOUniverse**, but patterns left unaddressed will cause deformation to your **YOUniverse**. If you do not break the old patterns, you are conflicting with your commands while manifesting the **YOUniverse**.

Let's say that every time you pay for a course to upgrade yourself, you feel negative; you feel like losing money, and you feel bad about it, but in contrast, you are expecting to learn as much as possible from that course that you bought with negative emotion.

Isn't it perplexing to know what to do? Should you be feeling sad about purchasing the course? Or should you be getting the most out of it? If you answer, "Learn the maximum because I gave away a lot of money to it," you are roughly squeezing a cow's udder to extract the maximum milk out of it.

You will either get kicked by the injured cow or injure the cow to the point where you will never get milk again, sooner or later.

Let's try this now: when you are paying for a course to upgrade yourself, smile and be grateful for sharing the knowledge in exchange for that energy called money. Look at the value exchange you are going to receive after investing the amount you did. Yes, I invested, but I did not pay for it or give it away.

Investing is associated with future outcome expectations, which is what we want in a course we are enrolling ourselves in, isn't it? Then why use different terminology and confuse everything and everyone, including you?

Break old patterns that are in conflict with your desired YOUniverse and the new patterns you want to form. By doing so, you are creating a new person out of yourself who is now freshly capable of handling a new phase of life without any baggage from the past, which is equally important as the former.

Step 7: Repeat the steps again.

"It is not the mountain we conquer, but ourselves."
-Dale Carnegie (1884-1962)
American author, Lecturer, and Self-Improvement
Expert.

By repeating, I mean not literally doing the same things again; we already covered that part in the respective steps wherever it is needed, but this repeating means finding a different area of life or maybe the same area of life with much more details with the new knowledge you gained. Or, even better, setting a higher goal than before and gradually and steadily raising the bar.

In my own life, I did this. I was earning around 50-60K per month from my job when I manifested 1L per month within a year, and once I was confident that the **YOUniverse** was conspiring to help me, I raised the bar and manifested 1.5L per month through my job within the next 6 months.

Once you master these steps, you will get the kick of doing them again and again in every possible aspect of life and playing the game again and again.

As I told you, everything in your **YOUniverse** is abundantly available; you don't have to suffocate your neighbor just to breathe more today, and similarly, you don't have to think that to make those extra bucks, you must squeeze someone out of their savings.

These are the seven steps to successfully manifesting anything you want in your life into your **YOUniverse**. Remember, this is your **YOUniverse**, and you have all the control over it. Your desire is a command, and the whole **YOUniverse** conspires to get you what you desire.

If in case you are looking for hand-held support from me, you can reach me at OmkaraCheerala.com or Google Omkara Cheetrala.

Please subscribe to my Author Page on Amazon so you shall be informed about the coming parts of this 7 books series inside which I will be revealing the secrets of '**The Zeroth Apple**' exclusively for each area of life in detail.

Summary

- ❖ This whole universe is filled with patterns.

- ❖ Nature has answers to all the questions we have.

- ❖ Patterns are not just interesting; they are groundbreaking.

- ❖ **Step 1:** Define your **YOUniverse**.

- ❖ **Step 2:** Write it down.

- ❖ **Step 3:** Assign an emotion to your desire.

- ❖ **Step 4:** Talk, Walk and Behave as if you already pose what you desire.

- ❖ **Step 5:** Identify Patterns and Inject them.

- ❖ **Step 6:** Break the current patterns.

- ❖ **Step 7:** Repeat the steps again.

BONUS CHAPTER:
HOW NOT TO CREATE YOUR
YOUNIVERSE.

By now you should have got all the value you wish to get from this book for the exchange of energy you invested. But as I said earlier, I am known for under promising and overdelivering. In this book, I couldn't deliver results but at least I could share you some extra nuggets to get you the best results.

So, I decided to give you a Bonus Chapter. When I say Bonus, it isn't some extra page fillers but something **important** and crucial in manifesting your YOUniverse and understanding **"The Zeroth Apple Concept"** further better.

After reading this Bonus Chapter, if you still feel like you need some hand holding, you can surely get in touch with me.

Google "Omkara Cheetrala" or reach out to me on OmkaraCheetrala.COM

Bannister's Story

On a sunny May afternoon in 1954, a young British runner named Roger Bannister stepped onto the track at Oxford University's Iffley Road stadium, his heart pounding with excitement and determination. He had trained for years for this moment, pouring all of his energy and focus into preparing for the race that would change his life forever.

As the starter's gun fired, Bannister took off at a breakneck pace, his long strides eating up the distance as he chased after the 4-minute barrier that had long eluded him. He could feel the eyes of the crowd on him, cheering him on as he pushed himself to the limit.

With every step he took, Bannister felt his heart pounding in his chest, urging him on to greater heights. He knew that this was the moment he had been working towards for so long, and he was not about to let it slip away.

As he approached the final stretch of the race, Bannister could feel the finish line drawing nearby. He put on a burst of speed, his feet pounding against the track as he pushed himself to the very limit.

And when he crossed the finish line in a time of 3 minutes, and 59.4 seconds, the crowd erupted in cheers and applause. Bannister had done it—he had run a mile in under 4 minutes, breaking a barrier that many had thought was impossible to overcome.

As he collapsed to the ground in exhaustion, Bannister knew that he had made history. He had achieved the impossible, and in doing so, he had inspired millions of people around the world to chase their own dreams and never give up.

"The only way to change the limiting beliefs you have about yourself is to change the way you think."
-Dr. John DeMartini
Keynote Speaker, Author, and Educator

News of Bannister's accomplishment spread around the world, "Roger Bannister, the first person to break the 4-minute mile barrier, ran the distance in a time of 3 minutes and 59.4 seconds on May 6, 1954. This was a significant accomplishment at the time, as it had long been thought that running a mile in under 4 minutes was not physically possible for a human being."

Records were created to be broken.

But Bannister's record stood for just over 46 days before it was broken by Australian runner John Landy on June 21, 1954.

On June 21, 1954, Landy took to the track at the Commonwealth Games in Vancouver, determined to beat Bannister's record and become the new holder of the 4-minute mile. As the starter's gun fired, Landy, burst out of the blocks and quickly settled into a fast pace.

The crowd watched in awe as Landy flew around the track, he could feel the pressure of the record bearing down on him, but he refused to let it get to him. He was focused and determined, and he knew that he had what it took to achieve greatness.

When he crossed the finish line in a time of 3 minutes, and 57.9 seconds, the crowd erupted in cheers and applause. Landy had done it—he had run a mile in under 4 minutes, breaking Bannister's record and becoming the new holder of the 4-minute mile.

Once a limiting belief system is broken, the results explode.
-Omkara Cheetrala
Indian Author cum Speaker

The story does not end here.

Jim Ryun of the United States, who ran a mile in 3 minutes and 51.3 seconds in 1967, and

Steve Ovett of Great Britain, who ran a mile in 3 minutes and 48.8 seconds in 1979,

Today, the mile record is held by Moroccan runner Hicham El Guerrouj, who ran a mile in 3 minutes, 43.13 seconds in 1999.

But the most important point I want to make here isn't yet clear. Do you know why I was inspired to document this story in my book—not because this is a historical record? For that matter, there are many historical records, to name a few:

1. **Fastest marathon time:** The current record for the fastest marathon time is held by Eliud Kipchoge of Kenya, who ran a marathon in 2 hours, 1 minute, and 39 seconds in 2019.

2. **Fastest 100-meter dash:** The current record for the fastest 100-meter dash is held by Usain Bolt of Jamaica, who ran the distance in 9.58 seconds in 2009.

3. **Most Grand Slam titles in tennis:** The current record for the most- 'Grand Slam titles in tennis is held by Roger Federer of Switzerland, who has won a total of 20 Grand Slam titles during his career.

4. **Most home runs in a single baseball season:** The current record for the most home runs in a single baseball season is held by Barry Bonds of the United States, who hit 73 home runs in 2001.

5. **Most NBA championships:** The current record for the most NBA championships is held by the Boston Celtics, who have won a total of 17 championships throughout their history.

Why Bannister?

But why only Banister's story? The answer lies in the story before Bannister broke the record. Till June 21st, 1954, pulmonologists (lung specialists) claimed that it was impossible to run at 15 miles per hour for 1.6 kilometers because our lungs aren't made to breathe such air, filter enough oxygen, and deliver the same into the blood at that rapid rate of breathing.

Cardiologists (heart specialists) debated whether the heart is designed to pump blood at such a high rate to legs, hands, eyes, the brain, and limbs simultaneously if someone attempted to run at 24.14 kmph.

And musculoskeletal specialists (muscle experts) argued that our muscles, ligaments, joints, fats, and other muscular elements in the human body aren't made to contract at that pace and release healthily if someone even attempts to make such rapid footwork.

Everyone believed and told them not to risk doing this except one person, and the rest is history. Today, we have record holders after record holders proving that those medical claims are nothing more than limited beliefs.

Guess what, Mr. Bannister died at the age of 88 on March 3, 2018, and definitely not because of any muscular or cardiac issues or because of lung concerns while running.

"Limiting beliefs are nothing more than a state of mind that you have adopted at some point in your life. They are not facts; they are only thoughts that you have chosen to believe."
- Dr. Joe Dispenza
New York Times best-selling Author, American chiropractor, International Lecturer, Researcher, and Educator in the fields of neuroscience, epigenetics, and quantum physics.

Guidelines on how not to Manifest.

With this new knowledge you got, let's get into "How not to create your YOUniverse."

Guideline 1: Creating with doubt.

Please do not try to create your YOUniverse with disbelief or doubt. I have enough students who have mastered all the techniques I taught them, be it NLP, the Law of Attraction, the Self-Hypnosis methods, EFT Tapping, or the Subconscious Mind Paradigm Shift, but they still live the same mediocre life just because of a little disbelief or a little voice in the back of their heads that keeps on telling them, "Hey! "This is too good to be true," "This has never been done before, so you won't be able to do it either."

I had a student in particular who wanted to learn everything related to the Enneagram from me. I found her enthusiasm impressive, and I agreed too. She started learning about the Basic Enneagrams, but then she had a doubt if this was truly a parameter to access human nature.

I explained to her that this is not an accurate absolute measure of human nature; there are others that should be bundled into a cluster, and only then can we identify a person's nature.

She became interested in the others now, the Tri-Types. I tried to explain to her that what she is doing is far worse than not learning anything, but she didn't listen to me yet and isn't ready to complete the study of the Enneagrams just because she has a doubt if this works.

"The only limitations you have are the limitations you believe."
-Maxwell Maltz (1899-1975)
Plastic Surgeon, Author, and Motivational Speaker

There is no such thing in this universe or in your **YOUniverse** that would work for all, as everything changes constantly and continuously, if that works, it defies **"The Law of Perpetual Transmutation of**

Energy" which falls off the guide rails of Rule 1 to create our YOUniverse.

Guideline 2: Creating with Confusion and Conflictions.

Imagine that your YOUniverse is a waiter at a hotel who understands only the menu items but no other language. When you went to that hotel, you wanted to order your favorite dosa, but instead, you said, "I don't want idly, I don't want chapati, and I also don't want any cool drinks; I only want Dosa.

Guess what will be served? Idly, chapati, cool drinks, and dosa Why? You asked for it. You can't say, "It is not what I ordered; maybe, but it is how it works."

Focus on only what you want; know what you don't want and keep it aside, not needing to speak about it or announce it, just being aware of it.

In reality, our desires always conflict. Let me show you how. We all want to be rich, but when we see rich people, we associate them with greed, cheating, bribery, and fake, bad emotions. Now, even if you manifested riches in your **YOUniverse**, you would now be that greedy cheater in your mind that you don't want, and you would shed all the riches that came to you.

This is true and is all around us. Have you ever heard of a lucky person winning the lottery, and within a month or so, he went back and broke into the same lifestyle, or even worse, met with an accident in which the amount he won was all spent?

"The mind is the cause of all things. It is the mind that creates the universe."
- Upanishads (Brihadaranyaka 4.4.5)

The depth of your emotions determines how much you can have them, and the feeling of that emotion determines how long you will have them, even if you get them by chance.

Guideline 3: Trying to understand "The Law of Paradox".

The Law of Paradox: This law states that everything is both true and not true at the same time. I agree that this law sounds very similar to the concept that we are articulating here. **YOUniverse'** s fundamental concept is founded on two theories that are closely related to this law.

However, if you wish to get the most out of your **YOUniverse** and manifest your desires, you should believe in one thing at a time. Believe it or not, if you start to doubt, you are going into the spiral of Guideline 1, and if you are confused and conflicts with yourself, you have again entered the spiral of Guideline 2.

But if you ask me, does my concept follow this law? The answer is a big yes. Everything you desire exists in the universe but not in your **YOUniverse**.

Just like I mentioned, for you to breathe more, you don't have to suffocate someone; there is enough air outside there beyond what you can consume in one shot. Similarly, the universe has more abundance than you can consume in a single lifetime. There is no scarcity in abundance unless you think there is.

Not only that, but this law is true in other senses also: It is true that you are going to manifest everything into your **YOUniverse** right now at the same time, but it is also not true that you do not have any of them in your **YOUniverse** right now.

"A disciplined mind leads to happiness, and an undisciplined mind leads to suffering."
-Buddha (563 BCE -483 BCE)
Founder of Buddhism

So, to wrap things up, don't try to over-understand "The Law of Paradox" too much in your **YOUniverse** and get stuck in a spiral of analysis paralysis.

We're here to manifest what we want; we're certain of it, and we don't want anything to confuse, contradict, or even slightly divert our attention, do we? Then let us do only that.

Guideline 4: Trying to create someone else's YOUniverse.

As I've said in other chapters, you can try to make a **YOUniverse** for someone, but keep in mind that it may be the best and most perfect one for them, but they won't be able to accept it if they can't accept it for themselves.

I call this the Honeybee Queen concept. It is applicable everywhere: in leadership, in love, in organizations, in management—everywhere people and emotions are involved.

If a hive of honeybees lost its queen, the bees disperse and die sooner, so usually, the harvesters purchase some queen bees and put them inside the hive carefully. But just by doing so, nobody can guarantee the lives of these bees or the life of that queen bee.

Yes, you read that right. If the male bees were not ready to accept this queen bee, they would kill her, tearing her body into pieces that even the harvester couldn't identify later. On the other hand, if they accept the queen, they build a queen's hive and then serve her forever.

This is exactly what you would be doing to your beloved ones if you tried to create a **YOUniverse** for them that they could not well resonate with; that **YOUniverse** would tear them apart emotionally, mentally, psychologically, and even physically.

Let everyone be their own creators in **YOUniverse**. If you really want someone to understand the power of **YOUniverse**, show them the results by applying them to yourself. Be the torchbearer for their lives. If you think you have manifested a significant **YOUniverse** into your life and they are not noticing it yet, do not worry, but understand that it is not yet the time for them.

"A strong man cannot help a weaker unless that weaker is willing to be helped, and even then, the weak man must become strong of himself; he must, by his own efforts, develop the strength which he admires in another."
-James Allen (1864-1912)
British Philosophical Writer

Until the time comes, not even the supreme conscious could help anyone without their approval.

Guideline 5: Arguing with someone who doesn't understand the concept.

Arguing is the last thing to do, or even if you ask me, I'd say that shouldn't be on your list at all. Arguing never brings positive emotions or feelings into your life. An argument, by definition, is a discussion or dispute in which reasons for and against a proposition or proposal are advanced between two people or a group of people who hold opposing opinions and belief systems and their ramifications.

So, it is apparent that the other person or group of people with whom you are trying to argue believes in something you can't see, just like they can't see what you have to offer. You would never enter an argument if you were ready to listen to their point of view, but if you are only listening to respond, you are essentially preparing a war ground for an argument, which never ends in peace without making the other person feel low, bad, or small.

Now, even if you win an argument by making them feel small, what did you achieve? In reality, you lost a person for life, and you could never teach them this concept in the entirety of your life at all.

Will you ever talk to someone openly, confidently, and with compassion about someone who made you feel small, bad, or wrong? So why do it to someone else?

Many of my students who don't want to stray from Guideline 5 enter Guideline 4 without realizing it, attempting to create a **YOUniverse** for those they don't want to argue with. Now that you've read Guideline 4 and Guideline 5, I'm sure you're smart enough not to break any of these rules.

"You will never win an argument, either you lose it or the person"
-Earl Nightingale (1921-1989)
American motivational speaker, radio personality, and author.

Guideline 6: Explaining the concept to someone without implementing it on your own, first.

This is not only a guideline for your **YOUniverse** but for anything in life. Never demonstrate something that you know is incomplete; you would make things worse than before. I'm not talking about the most complicated things like surgery, rocketry, or even aeronautics; let's take something as simple as fixing your geyser at home, which you don't fully understand and try to fix; either you give your kids a shock touching that tap that you thought fixed them, or you become paranoid about whether you ever fixed it correctly. Every scream that comes from that bathroom would fill you with guilt if something bad happened as a result of something you didn't do.

I'm not saying you shouldn't demonstrate or speak about this book; all I'm saying is don't do it until you've mastered the concept.

Assume you were hungry and came to my house, where I was expecting you not so early. I realized that you were hungry, and so I pulled the food from the oven just past half-time of its baking or frying. I love you, and I don't want to see you suffer from hunger, so I rushed through the process without checking if the rice was fully cooked or the curry was fully prepared, and I didn't even notice if the dishes were properly cleaned.

I love you; I can't bear the thought of you feeling hungry, so I did everything for you and served the half-cooked food on a half-cleaned plate; would you like it? Can you or someone or even anyone dare to have it? Maybe let me ask it this way: can someone consume it and still be, okay? Consider how their gut would react if it was half-baked or cooked.

Isn't it the same as what you are doing if you decide to explain this concept without knowing everything for yourself first?

Or perhaps this time, the rice is properly cooked, and everything is perfect, but I didn't check the taste; I am unsure about the spice level, salt level, and taste, and I served you; even so, you may not enjoy the food at the level it requires. I could serve you the food without assessing the taste if I became an expert in what I was cooking, but not before that.

If you agree with what I am saying all this time, then even if you come across the temptation of asking your friend to read this book, control yourself until you become an expert in this concept. Maybe this way you'll actually force yourself to finish this book and put it into action. I wish my publisher didn't get upset by now because I am not speaking like a marketer because, for me, you are important but not for the energy exchange you give me in the form of some currency.

"The road to hell is paved with good intentions."
-Samuel Johnson (1709-1784)
British Literary Figure, Essayist, Lexicographer,
Poet, and Novelist

Guideline 7: Pushing someone to believe what you believe.

Never try to push someone to understand this concept and make the most of it. This is as similar to arguing with others; the only difference here is that in arguing, you argue with someone who believes in something else, whereas pushing is forcing someone who doesn't believe in this concept. There is not much separation between the two.

In fact, for that matter, I thought of adding this guideline as a small paragraph within Guideline 5 itself, but then while I was typing, I realized this is a widespread and possibly unintentional activity; we all do this at all times, and it requires a detailed explanation and, if possible, steps to avoid, so I wrote this down as a separate guideline.

Let me give you another example: Imagine I pet a horse and I love it so much that I treat it the same way I treat my children. Now I got her a refreshing drink recommended by the vet, who has seen hundreds of favourable results in horse health improvement across all of his consultations.

I got her this drink on a summer Sunday at noon, excited and with a lot of love; what do we all expect? It should too be responding with the same enthusiasm and love, right?

No, just because you've got the best for it doesn't mean it's the right time! You're not going to be able to feed my horse anything. On the contrary, if the horse is thirsty and the timing is just right, even if you pour it some normal tap water too, she will drink it with a grateful attitude.

A wise man once said, **"Time and persons of influence could change the intensity of something they say."** Your wife may never have listened to you when you said, "Don't slam the car door," but the day her girlfriend gives her a car to take care of, she will scream at you even if you close the car door like you used to. It depends on the right time, the right person, and the influence that person has on them. This is one of the reasons why great artists are just another member of the group for their family and friends. They never get to decide whatever they want, even a Supreme Court Magistrate is a father at home, and he has to bend down on his knees to be a horse for his Grand Children if asked for.

Summary

❖ Just because many say so doesn't make it the right thing to do.

❖ If others have failed, it does not follow that you will also fail.

❖ Once a limiting belief is broken, records explode.

❖ Never create your YOUniverse with self-doubt.

❖ Do not create your YOUniverse with confusion and conflicts!

❖ Avoid understanding too much of "The Law of Paradox."

❖ Stop trying to create someone else's **YOUniverse.**

❖ Arguing never helps you win anything; instead, it causes you to lose yourself in the process of arguing with the other person.

❖ Forcing someone to do or believe something that you do or believe is nothing less than domestic violence.

CONCLUSION:

To sum up, while we were all looking for some Aladdin's lamp, we forgot that we are the Genies of our lives and have the power to make our own **YOUniverses** happen.

This is not a book you can read once and then say you're a master of manifestation and could create whatever **YOUniverse** you want. Instead, read this book a second time with dedication and perform the actions mentioned in the book while going through it a third time.

To achieve the best results out of this book, make sure you read it the first time in a stretch within a week's time, the second time in 2 weeks' time, and the third time with actions under a month.

Always highlight the portions you liked during the first two passes that could help you in your implementation phase.

You could always keep this book as a reference for future use and never share it with anyone else, even the closest ones, as this isn't just a book but your energy and emotion.

APPENDIX:

THANK YOU:

Dear reader,

I am grateful for your interest in **"The Zeroth Apple – Manifest your Abundant YOUniverse."** I hope that this book has provided you with valuable insights to help you harness the power of your mind and spirit to achieve success and well-being.

I would also like to thank our families and loved ones for their support and encouragement throughout the writing process. Their unwavering belief in us and this project has been a source of inspiration and strength.

Finally, I am grateful for the opportunity to serve you, my readers. My goal has always been to help you live a more fulfilling life, and I hope that this book has contributed to that in some small way.

With gratitude,

Omkara Cheetrala